BEYOND CONSTANTINOPLE

The Memoirs of an Ottoman Jew

VICTOR ESKENAZI

I.B. TAURIS

LONDON · NEW YORK

Published in 2016 by
I.B.Tauris & Co. Ltd
London • New York
www.ibtauris.com

This edition taken from *Thanks for the Buggy Ride: Memoirs of an Ottoman Jew* published in Turkey by Libra Kitap in 2013

ISBN: 978 1 78453 266 6
eISBN: 978 0 85772 925 5

A full CIP record for this book is available from the British Library
A full CIP record is available from the Library of Congress

Library of Congress Catalog Card Number: available

Printed and bound in Sweden by ScandBook AB

VICTOR ESKENAZI was born in 1906 and raised in Ottoman Istanbul. He travelled throughout Europe in the 1920s, settling in Vienna and Italy. During World War II, he moved to London and worked for the British Intelligence Corps. An antique dealer by profession, he died in Milan in 1987.

'... the book gives off a sense of goodness and honour and one thing I found especially moving was his pride in being Jewish, in that it gave him a moral centre and code of ethics rather than ... [making] him part of a group possessed with special qualities. In fact, one senses strongly that he sees himself as part of a common humanity which aims at the pursuit of good.'

DONNA LEON author of the *Commissario Guido Brunetti* crime novels.

*When I was young there was a song called
"Thanks for the Buggy Ride".*[*]

It had a joyful lilt.

*The wonderment of a city dweller strolling
through beautiful countryside.*

*It sounded to me like a thanksgiving
for God's nature.*

A hymn to life.

---

[*] This epigraph is taken from the previous edition of this book, titled *Thanks for the Buggy Ride: Memoirs of an Ottoman Jew.*

Contents

List of Plates

Foreword

On a luminous dawn, one day in July 1965, I was standing on the prow of a cruise ship sailing majestically into the golden mist of the Bosphorus, straining my sleepy eyes in order to get my first glimpse of the fabled Istanbul, or Stamboul, or better still Constantinople as my elders would say, with a beatific smile on their face. This mythical realm, home to my family for centuries, was now only a few miles away and, although I had never been there, I felt like Ulysses returning to Ithaca.

My father came up to me silently, put his arm around my shoulder, hugged me and whispered, "Finally, here we are! All together in one of the most beautiful cities of the world, one of the great centres of civilisation, certainly the centre of our world for generations." He had tears in his eyes, and I knew it was not the wind.

Captain V.H. Eskenazi had not been back since he had been stationed here during World War II as a British Intelligence officer and this was going to be the first of many return visits right up to the time of his death.

Victor, or Victoriko as his mother called him or Tori as his sister would address him, was the product of a world that has now disappeared. He was a typical representative of the religious and ethnic minorities that thrived in an urban milieu during Ottoman times and that were of fundamental importance to the success of the Empire because of their role in commerce, administration, culture, science and international relations. These groups tended to include very interesting people, frequently eccentrics (we had many such examples in our family), eager to make a better life for themselves. They were also entrepreneurial and inventive, with a great sense of belonging to their community and the city that was their home.

Young Victor was born in 1906 and lived with his mother and father, and his sister, Jenny, in a huge *yali*[1] in Beylerbey, with his extended family of almost fifty members ruled over by their grandfather. He used to recount how on Saturdays, the whole family would eat together and the children would go in turn to kiss the hand of the wise old man. After his grandfather died the family dispersed and mostly settled in Galata, and the *yali* has sadly since burned down.

---

[1] *Yali*: a waterside residence in Istanbul, overlooking the Bosphorus.

The beginning of the twentieth century was a very critical period in Ottoman history. It witnessed not only the end of the Empire and the defeat in World War I, but also the presence of the victorious allied armies and the wave of White Russians fleeing the Revolution, which added to the already highly cosmopolitan nature of Constantinople. Victor breathed the complex air of this budding new Turkey with its ideals, contradictions, demagogies and hopes. He always felt blessed to have been born at such an extraordinary moment in history and was obsessed with the idea of narrating his colourful experiences as a young man in Istanbul in order to pass them on to the next generations. I thank him for having done so.

If I really had to define my father, a man of various facets and many incarnations, I would primarily identify him as an Ottoman seigneur. Ottoman because of his inbred cosmopolitanism, his wide vision of the world, his insatiable intellectual curiosity, his instinctive understanding and respect of other peoples, cultures and behaviours, and when required also a determination and assertiveness that is so prevalent in the Ottoman personality and in the history of its Empire. Seigneur – and I insist on this slightly obsolete French term – not only because he was from a francophone milieu, but also because of his *savoir faire*, charm, elegance and the ability to be at ease with everybody and make everybody else feel at ease in his presence. Moreover, I cannot forget his love for French literature – *Cyrano de Bergerac* being a particular favourite – which he would recite too emphatically, causing deep embarrassment to us children.

To all of this, one would have to add a very British connotation acquired at school and in the army and enhanced by his red hair, freckles and fair complexion. V.H., as he was known during his military days, had an overdeveloped sense of fair play, a very pragmatic way of dealing with adversities, and a profound sense of duty and responsibility that privilege and power had granted him. One inherited British passion was tennis, at which he excelled, unlike the playing of American songs on the guitar, at which he definitely did not. Another was his perverse passion for scrambled eggs and kippers, not to mention Marmite!

Having spent a large part of his life in Italy, Vittorio had also naturally adopted a sunny optimism and a certain theatrical mannerism, which added to his affable personality.

But above all Victor Ben Haim was fundamentally a Sephardi Jew, intimately proud of his ancient, open-minded tradition of al-Andalus and respectful of its ethical principles. Born into a family in which religious ritual was very marginal, his sense of moral obligation and duty to family and community were deeply rooted in Jewish thought, and throughout his complex life he was guided by an impregnable sense of justice that made him always full of gratitude towards the Creator. In later years, he became one of the wise men of the Jewish community in

Milan and very much sought after for his benevolent advice.

My father started writing his book in the final years of his life, at home in his studio, sitting at his narrow desk, informal in his elegant dressing gown, and using his old Parker pen and turquoise ink to cram small sheets of paper with his flowing cursive as he sipped coffee with a fulfilled, inward smile on his face. After so many years of gestation he was at long last writing his memoirs, now in a great hurry cutting corners, but at the same time desperately trying to slow down the flow of thoughts and recollections that had been patiently waiting in his brain to finally pour out onto the page.

He skipped entirely the more bourgeois, later part of his life and only briefly mentioned his beloved Laure, his dedicated wife for over fifty-two years; he also omitted his success as an antique dealer in Italy, his prominent role within Milanese society and in the Jewish community. Nor did he mention my sister Peggy and myself, such a fundamental part of his "buggy ride" and the focus of his attention and affection. Fundamentally Victor was a very private, reserved man when it came to family matters and he rarely expressed his innermost sentiments publicly.

He had the habit of reading me passages of the book he was particularly pleased with, not so much for my approval, but somehow to reconnect with moments of a life so different and remote, he somehow was not sure it had been his own.

Initially I was not very enthusiastic about his endeavour, as I worried he was speeding up his work as though he felt there was very little time left. In these last years he had suffered from heart problems and, as I dreaded, he died of a heart attack in 1987, a month after his book was published in Italian, aged eighty-one, still energetic and young in spirit.

At home our family jargon was very picturesque and not always comprehensible, as we jumped from one language to another. The official tongue was French, although Italian was more and more present; English was spoken when discussing school matters and later on business, but there were also plenty of Ladino sayings, a sprinkle of Turkish words, frequently referring to food, while Greek swear words, taught to me at an early age, were the rule. Consequently my father's very proper, slightly old-fashioned Italian text seemed to me not to convey the liveliness, charm and confusion that were so characteristic of our family life. I was wrong. The book was an unexpected success.

My father appreciated languages above everything else, even more than general knowledge or history, which were both very much his passion. He insisted his mother tongue was Greek because of the nannies and servants in his household. His parents spoke French, the lingua franca of the upper classes, especially around the Mediterranean, and Ladino, the medieval Spanish of the Sephardi Jews. According to family tradition, he was schooled at the German School in Istanbul during World War I. But being thin, Jewish and a British subject he was regularly beaten up, until he learned to box, rather too late, and he was soon sent to the English High School for Boys, now Anadolu Lisesi in Nisantasi. He was privately tutored in Turkish of course, which he could write in the Ottoman script, and in Russian and Hebrew; Italian he learned last. With the exception of Hebrew, he could speak all of these languages perfectly and write beautifully in most of them; quite an achievement, but one that was not uncommon among the urban minorities of that period. Surprisingly, however, and to his great frustration, he could never master the Milanese dialect! Whatever the language, he was in the habit of interjecting his speech with *"inshallah"* or *"mashallah"*, which at times could be very embarrassing, especially in the company of pious Catholics or Jews. This idiosyncrasy was happily adopted by all the family, including myself and to this day. In a way, I think he was asserting his deep-rooted belonging to a Middle Eastern cosmos.

He managed to write an English and a French version of his book and had started the German text when he passed away. I remember distinctly how displeased he was with himself as his Turkish was too rusty to complete a version in that language too, since he longed for the modern-day inhabitants of Istanbul to savour the exuberance and vibrancy of their unique city at the time of his youth.

Istanbul is now a very different place. In these last decades of profound change his memories have mutated from intense reality to faded myth.

The city has now almost twenty times the inhabitants it used to have and has had to adapt to the frequently misunderstood necessities of modernity, development and the obsession of economic growth. High levels of immigration and hordes of oblivious tourists in trainers now populate the historic Istanbul, once home to a picturesque crowd of elegant administrators of the Empire, religious officials, merchants from every corner of the earth, extraordinary craftsmen, soldiers of every rank and uniform and swarms of poor people worn by the hardness of survival.

Vestiges of Constantinople's varied and refined architecture are now besieged by the new city and are frequently left to decay to make space for new developments or else over-manicured for the pressing needs of tourism. Hidden away in untouched corners, the soul of the city thankfully lingers on.

Whenever I visit Istanbul I sense a return to my most profound roots, an idealised family history in an idealised, intense, genuine and joyous world. Somehow I feel I have genetically inherited my father's familiarity with his Constantinople. I wander around in a state of elation, in and out of the present, mixing my own experiences with those of my departed family. On turning a corner, I get a glimpse of my mother on a buggy being taken to school, I imagine a young Victor leaving his home (now a hotel) for his tennis club, beaming with pride, wearing his brand new white V-neck pullover, my uncle diving in the Bosphorous with his friends; my great uncle visiting patients followed by his towering Albanian body guard; my petite aunt buying flowers at Ciçek Passaje, my grandmother choosing the perfect fish for the evening meal.

Smells are certainly the same as in the past and enhance my state of trance. The decaying, salty odour of fish, the combined fumes of coal, ferry boats, shish kebab and cigarettes, the scent of linden trees, lemon cologne, spices and the all-pervading whiffs of cooking that instantly sit me at my mother's table in Milan.

The sounds, I am sure, are also the same, the large boats bumping against the piers, their disquieting hoots competing with the cries of the seagulls, the rattling of the tramways, the cries of the vendors, the touching calls to prayer of the muezzins, painfully longing for the love of the Divine, the rumble of the language I do not speak, but which somehow speaks to me with its guttural undertones.

Who knows, maybe in my cycle of rebirths, sometime in the course of history, hopefully, I was also born in Constantinople, a velvet weaver, an astronomer, a foreign merchant or as a *hamal*, carrying huge weights up and down the narrow streets of Galata, bent in two, a walking pyramid of goods. My father's childhood dream.

I am never melancholic, just pervaded by a languorous longing for a paradisiacal past totally influenced by the freshness and ardour of my father's writing, the irreplaceable fullness of some periods of his life that he needed to pass on, a connection to a magical reality he knew he had been blessed with. But above all, I am grateful for having left behind his well-inhabited cosmopolitanism, a sort of belvedere terrace looking over the city, from where one can observe, understand and embrace every culture, human behaviour and belief with a heart full of curiosity, wonderment and joy.

I hope the fragrance of this universal vision will intoxicate the reader, reaching straight to the heart.

John Eskenazi
London

Chapter One

I knocked softly at the door.

"Come in," said my guardian.

I entered his study, shutting the door carefully behind me, so as not to make any noise. The lamp on the desk shed a greenish light all over the room, casting weird shadows on the walls. He was writing and lifted his head as I came in, looking at me above his spectacles.

"Sit down," he said, a softness in his voice.

The chair in front of his desk was too tall and my legs were dangling above the floor.

"Your mother tells me you have again broken the pane of glass in the hall, playing football."

I was looking down, avoiding his eyes, as still as a mouse.

"It is right you should play at your age, but you must start to think before you get yourself into mischief. You are not a child any more."

I had just turned seven.

"You see, my boy," he continued, his face shining with all the goodness for which people loved him, "broken panes cost money and have to be replaced, and what we throw away we cannot give to the poor."

My guardian was a physician and there was always somebody asking for help at our door.

My father had just died. My mother, my sister and I lived in my guardian's and aunt's house. He was my father's elder brother and my aunt was my mother's sister. My aunt had never had children and we were looked upon as belonging to the household. I was less saddened by the loss of my father than by the attitude of relatives and friends who did not conceal their compassion for us, poor orphans.

My uncle acted as a father to me, a duty I think he had always wished to share with his brother. My sister and I were always cherished by him as if we were his own children. In return I gave him my deepest affection and his word was, and has ever been for me, a source of enlightenment and a guide to the way I think.

We lived in a vast apartment house on the third floor of a large building, in the European quarter of Constantinople, as Istanbul was called in those days. It was a very particular city, inhabited by people of very varied origin. One would hear a babel of tongues walking through its streets and meet foreigners from all parts of the world.

Constantinople, in those days, represented the bridge between East and West. The navel of the

Earth. A wondrous and fascinating place to live. Its long-established foreign residents in the European quarter gave it a progressive, cosmopolitan aspect, very much in accordance with the international way of life of the period, but nevertheless, over the years, contact with the philosophy and charm of Oriental life had strongly influenced their way of thinking.

At home we spoke French. With my uncle, who had studied gynaecology at Leipzig, I spoke German. I was going then to a German school and had to get familiar with the language. Foreign children did not frequent Turkish elementary schools. The method of teaching was too different.

The year was 1915 and, as a partner in the Triple Alliance, Turkey was on the side of Germany and Austro-Hungary against the Allies. Since the beginning of the war, all French, English and later Italian schools had been closed and I had no alternative.

I spoke Ladino with my maternal grandmother. She did not know any other language. The few Turkish words she could muster talking to the janitor or street vendors were rather approximate. I also used the same language with the old woman who came to do the washing on Mondays.

Ladino, the characteristic idiom spoken by the Jews who were exiled from Spain during the Inquisition at the end of the fifteenth century, was at that time still in its purest form: archaic Spanish interspersed with Hebrew words and enriched with translated Hebrew maxims. Its pristine flavour had not yet been adulterated by an admixture of Turkish, Greek, French and even Slavic words.

Until the age of two I had only spoken Greek because my nanny, like the majority of female servants in European households in Constantinople, came from the Greek islands of the Dodecanese.

Our manservant, who was also my guardian's bodyguard when he had to go out at night to attend a patient in childbirth, was an Albanian *kawas*.[2] True to his race and his profession, he was awe-inspiring in appearance when bedecked in his traditional garb and weaponry. He lived very much on his own at the far end of the corridor leading into the entrance hall. His small room looked like a guard post. His rifle hung over his camp bed, and his revolver and *yataghan*[3] were always on a stool, within arm's reach, ready to do battle at any moment. Although very much afraid of his warlike paraphernalia, I was fascinated by his weapons and always tried to find an excuse to go and call on him, in his room, so as to get a glimpse of his arsenal.

This faithful Albanian, clad in his distinctive costume, with revolver and *yataghan* clearly visible in the wide red woollen sash he wore around his waist, sat on the box at the coachman's side, as my guardian's carriage careered through empty streets, in the deep of the night. Most neighbourhoods were safe but the sight of a bellicose Albanian was apt

---

[2] *Kawas*: a bodyguard.
[3] *Yataghan*: a type of Ottoman knife or short sabre.

to discourage any felonious attacks by marauding toughs.

It seemed to me quite uncanny that so many women chose to bring forth their offspring into the world at some ungodly hour between midnight and early dawn. There were few nights when I was not dragged from my sleep by the insistent trill of the doorbell, pulsing under the energetic thumb of an anxious father-to-be. For many years, after my guardian's death, I woke up suddenly at night sometimes, having dreamed I heard the insistent, pitiless ring of a doorbell.

At the tender age of eight I had already made up my mind as to what I wanted to do as a grown-up. To be a *kawas* like my uncle's bodyguard was certainly a very attractive prospect because of those fascinating weapons, but I was also tremendously impressed by the gigantic *hamals*. These powerful porters carried incredible burdens up the steep gradients of the old city. Bent almost double under the weight of a steel safe or a piano, supported on their backs by a sort of pack-saddle fastened by strong braces under their armpits, they heaved themselves slowly up the streets, resting awhile when the projecting corner of a wall offered them an opportunity to ease the weight on their shoulders. Then, bathed in perspiration, they brought a lazy hand to their forehead and with a sudden lightning backhand swipe, they would splash a pool of sweat on the pavement in front of their feet. How could such an extraordinary performance fail to impress a well-behaved youngster constrained to use a hand-kerchief to wipe his brow?

As I look back into my childhood, images, sounds and sensations surge vividly into my mind from the depths of my memory. Every night, as my sister and I fell into sleep in the darkness of our bedroom, we heard the bark of the street dogs. A long howl would give the signal from some far-off back alley and then like wildfire all the dogs in the neighbourhood would join in the deafening chorus. These vagrant mongrels infested all quarters of the city. In daytime they would sleep in some half-hidden corner, as if trying not to be noticed, but at night they assembled in packs and roamed the streets with bared fangs and bristling hair.

As the barking of the dogs reached a climax we would hear the metallic sound of bolts being drawn and the housewives would open their street doors. The loud banging of tin cans against the pavement and a noise like wet rags being thrown down would indicate that the culinary waste of the household had been strewn all over the street. In a few moments the barking would change key and assume a joyful pitch.

Now and again a rending howl would disturb the harmony. A weaker animal had been cast out by the sharp teeth of his stronger fellows. With the end of the banquet the turmoil would cease. Although, here and there, the sound of gnawing teeth on a forgotten bone would still break the silence. Then finally, the muted sound of shuffling paws would herald the retreat. The mongrel pack would vanish from sight and revert to its hidden refuge. The quiet of the night would settle on the streets, now clean of every trace of refuse.

We children would fall into deep slumber. The barking of the dogs did not greatly disturb us, we were so used to it. Sometimes, in the middle of the night, I would wake up suddenly. The silence in the house would frighten me and I strained my ears lest I should hear some suspicious noise. Then, almost imperceptible, from the far-off drawing room at the other end of our apartment, I would distinguish the friendly, familiar ticking of our large mantel clock. The sound would dispel my anxiety and lull me back to sleep.

When one of the usual seasonal fires broke out on a summer night an eerie call, echoing all over the neighbourhood would rouse us from our sleep. *"Yanghin var, yanghin vaaar..."* (There's a fire). The nightwatchman pounding his heavy iron-shod club on the cobblestones would utter his dismal cry drawing out the last syllable so plaintively as to make one's blood curdle. We would lie still in our beds until we heard the grown-ups walking about the house. The news of the fire created tremendous agitation throughout the apartment houses and young and old would rush up the stairs to the terrace on top of the building to watch its progress.

Looking out of the windows the reddening of the sky seemed right above our neighbourhood, but it was generally the wooden houses in the crowded popular suburbs that were burning. As the aubergines ripened and were sold off cheaply in the markets, fires became a common occurrence with whole districts, thousands of ramshackle wooden houses, burning uncontrollably for days on end. The cooking in these poorer households was usually done on rickety, four-legged box-like iron contraptions, which were easily upset. The frying pans, containing the savoury vegetables cooking in oil, would fall onto the burning charcoal and the old wooden houses would go up like tinder. As bad luck would have it there always seemed to be a favourable wind to spread the flying sparks in every direction, starting small fires here and there, which would then merge into a sea of flames. From our vantage point we could hear the crackle and the smell of the burning wood and feel the heat, like a tremendous brazier. The sight was terrifying but still the danger was far away and we all went back to our beds after a time.

In the apartment buildings of the European quarters a part of the roof consisted of a large open-air terrace and a series of covered laundry rooms, which smelled pleasantly of good soap, where tenants could attend to their weekly washing. These large rooms and the terraced areas where the washing was hung up to dry became the undisputed realm of the children on non-laundry days when there were no gruff washerwomen about and no snow-white sheets waving in the wind. In these secluded precincts we children would learn to smoke our first cigarettes and play the usual games between boys and girls: "husband and wife" and "the doctor's visit." Strangely enough, we boys were always the patients to be visited. The girls acted as nurses, very proficiently. In time, one learned from the more forward playmates that newborn babies were not found in cabbage patches and that a girl was not irremediably put in the family way for having been kissed on the mouth by a boy.

The first noises to wake us from our early morning drowsiness were the plaintive bleating of the sheep herded towards the slaughterhouse and the dull sound of a rusty piece of tin beaten by the shepherd's crook to hasten the progress of the flock. The patter of the hooves on the cobblestones sounded like the flow of a mountain river. In their hundreds, these doomed animals were driven from their pastures on the hills surrounding the Golden Horn, up the incline edged by the massive city dwellings of our neighbourhood, and funnelled through the narrow side street below our bedroom windows. A few hundred yards further on, the poor animals were driven down a rough slope bordered by slanting, rickety, wooden dwellings, towards the shores of the Sea of Marmara, at the confluence with the Bosphorus. There they were slaughtered in dismal shacks, covered by rusty corrugated iron roofs, which defiled the landscape. Their sad lot filled our tender young hearts with great compassion.

As the first diligent housewives aired their bedding, the clamour of the itinerant vendors filled the street with characteristic and colourful cries. The most acute sound was the shriek of the Albanian who sold sheep's brain and feet. The brain was invisible, hidden under fig leaves in a wicker basket he carried under his arm. The sheep's feet, on the other hand, were very conspicuous. Bound together in small bunches, like asparagus and slung across the shoulders, like bandoliers, these blood-smeared, severed, diminutive limbs were very upsetting.

The deep-voiced call of the peasant who sold yoghurt was less overpowering. Two wide, round, low-rimmed tin platters, containing thick country yoghurt, were fastened by three cords at each end of a long pole he carried over his shoulders.

Running barefoot with a swinging gait, the itinerant fishmonger would balance a large wooden tray of silvery fish over his head. At his sharp cry, *"Balik"*,[4] the housewives would rush to their windows and a colourful exchange of scurrilous wit would ensue during their bargaining. The fishmongers, who were usually Sephardi Jews from the dockside, would use Ladino or very vernacular Greek. Strange to say, the sedate housewives could more than hold their own in these vociferous jousts (revealing a hidden talent with which they would never have been credited, judging solely by appearances).

Advancing majestically down the street the Greek vegetable and fruit vendor would appear in his turn, balancing his scales like an acolyte's censer. Behind

---

[4] *Balik*: fish

him, breathing heavily, his hefty young help would carry an immense basket, secured to his back, containing neatly ordered fruit and vegetables. Sometimes the carrying would be done by a small donkey pulling a light cart in which the merchandise could be displayed to better advantage. According to the time of the year, the scales, held at elbow's length, would contain skilfully arranged pyramids of golden apricots or dark red cherries. The various commodities on sale would be announced with precise and particular modulations, in demotic Greek.

A raucous call would issue from the parched throat of a robust Kurd as he plodded along, bent under the weight of a large pannier laden to the brim with melons and watermelons. All kind of hawkers, offering an endless variety of merchandise, each with his own traditional and distinctive cry, would follow one another down our street. There would be tinkers, knife-grinders, lace-vendors, artisans who could mend or manufacture virtually anything on the spot. The tinker would sit at a street corner and conjure on demand any culinary utensil out of an empty kerosene tin can he always carried on his back. With a pair of strong scissors, a hammer to beat down sharp edges and a bar of solder he would melt on a portable heater, he could produce anything from a washing tub to a frying pan. Empty tin cans, *téneke* as they were called, transforming the English "tin can" into the vernacular, were the most serviceable material across the whole country. It was always handy and easily available.

Among the vendors who filled the street in the morning, a singular character would at times make an appearance. Distinguishing himself from the rabble by his Mongol features, he would walk sedately through the crowd, clad in a magnificent, multicoloured, striped caftan, wearing a round, gold-embroidered cap on his completely shaven head. From time to time he would utter in Ladino a strange sing-song call *"Adobar cinis... adobar cinis"*, meaning he could repair porcelain and ceramics.

I have never been able to ascertain (as I tried to gain information on the subject in later years) why these strange, exotic wanderers, who roamed around Europe and the Orient plying their craft, used the same cry in every country they visited in the particular idiom of the Spanish Jews who had been exiled from Spain and had lived in Turkey since the end of the fifteenth century.

Originating from Chinese Turkestan, from Khotan or the Samarkand region, these clever artisans knew how to repair porcelain and ceramics in a very particular manner. Hailed from a window to do a job, the Turcoman would sit on the doorstep and wait for the broken pieces to be brought to him in order to examine them carefully, before deciding if he would undertake the repair, or not. On being satisfied that the separate pieces fitted together perfectly, the artisan extracted from the leather satchel, which hung at his side, a short bow, a small wooden-handled, diamond-tipped steel prong, a pair of small pincers, a ball of steel wire and a thin brush. Once the object had been pieced back together, the broken fragments would be marked at the necessary points where the work had to be started. Then, slinging the chord of the bow around the circular wooden head of the prong, the bow would be moved horizontally to and fro very swiftly producing a rotating motion, which would pierce the hard porcelain, the softer ceramic or earthenware, in a short time. When the pieces had been drilled, the Turcoman would ask the housewife for a fresh egg, which he would then separate. The edges of the broken pieces would be moistened with the brush, which had been previously dipped in egg white. This slightly adhesive substance would keep the broken segments momentarily together, until they could be secured by threading steel wire through the holes in perfect juxtaposition. The overlapping edges would then be cut with the pincers. Objects thus held together by small steel brackets would never come apart and I have seen antique porcelain and ceramic pieces repaired in this fashion centuries ago, still as solidly held together as on the day they were repaired by one of these extraordinary wandering craftsmen.

Such were the sights, the cries and the turmoil on the street below our windows in the early part of the morning when this usually peaceful, narrow road was transformed into a busy market. Money and goods were exchanged between the windows and the street by means of a basket attached to a long cord, which would go up and down vertiginously.

In this confusion and still chewing the last morsels of our breakfast, my sister and I would rush towards school, our satchels banging on our backs and swinging our small, plaited straw baskets, containing our break-time bread and butter rolls. My sister and I went to the same school. It was a French institute for girls but little boys were tolerated up to the age of seven. It is there I learned how to use a needle threaded with red wool, stitching elementary patterns on white, square-holed canvas, as I sat on a narrow bench, elbow-to-elbow with sniggering little girls who made fun of my clumsiness.

The toing and froing of street vendors and the confusion would come to a standstill in the afternoon when we were free from school. After our midday meal, we children would impatiently await the sing-song of the ice-cream vendor who appeared every day at the same hour, carrying two large containers swathed in white linen, slung to a stout, curved pole across his shoulders. We would run down the stairs with our empty glasses to have them filled with delicious plain ice cream or exquisite sorbets made with the fruit of the season, which tasted as if it had just been picked off the tree.

About teatime a subdued call would announce the arrival of the old woman who sold corncobs. She would sit on our doorstep and wait for us. Out of a large carrying bag made of woven straw she would produce small cobs of tender corn, which were kept boiling hot under layers of spotless white muslin. To make our meal more appetising she would conjure out of one of the deep pockets of her caftan a flat tin box containing salt crystals.

Now and again a jumble of voices would be heard coming from the main street as a crowd assembled on the pavement facing our building. Surrounded by a turbulent mob on each side of the road, two hard-faced characters, carrying large, boldly painted, tin containers on their backs, would be the centre of attraction. When the crowd had swelled to a sufficient size, the two mountebanks would start a mock quarrel in which they exchanged florid insults and scurrilous and allusive insinuations about the other's personal integrity, and not sparing for a moment the respectability of mothers, sisters, grandparents and ancestors, even those of each other's next-door neighbours. People would listen bemused to this flow of abuse, laughing their heads off, and trying to catch and remember some of the gems of bad language they heard, in order to turn it to good advantage when the occasion arose.

During studied pauses in the *tenzon*, containers would be opened, disgorging white clouds of candyfloss, which would be offered to the public comparing it to a candid bridal veil, a gift from heaven. The merry crowd would willingly spend a few coins for the entertainment and the sweet delicacy and the two smart fellows, satisfied with their business, would leave, side by side, for another street corner.

At an early age my sister and I were subjected to piano lessons as behove scions of families of good standing. Our teacher lived in one of those derelict wooden houses, completely askew, which seemed to remain upright by some miracle. Halfway down a steep descent, which ended near the dockyard, we would stop at a narrow terrace where a group of wooden three-storey houses stood leaning against each other. At the ring of a bell, pulled by a thin cord that hung at the side of the door, the dishevelled head of Fräulein von K. would appear at a top-storey window.

Our teacher was a very old German spinster of noble descent who gave piano lessons to eke out a meagre living. I do not know how my charitable guardian came to know of the poor woman's miserable circumstances, but it was certainly his desire to help her rather than his wish to encourage our musical talent that prompted him to gratify us with piano lessons. The mystery of the adverse circumstances that had brought this old gentlewoman to live in these sordid tenements was never solved.

The door-key would be slowly lowered to us, hanging on a much-knotted length of old string, and we would climb up the unsafe, creaking stairs. Fräulein von K. would wait at the door of her lodgings consisting of two small rooms in one of which an upright piano took up most of the wall space. The opposite wall of the room and both walls of her tiny bedroom were covered with a multitude of yellowing photographs reproducing the semblance of haughty personages. Ladies dressed in velvet and silk, covered with frills and laces, and gentlemen in officer's uniform on foot or horseback with gilt corselets and pointed helmets. On the front lawn of an imposing castle, a small figure elegantly attired in a white dress, shading herself with a lace parasol, stood nonchalantly leaning against a large wicker armchair. Was this aristocratic young lady our poor old music teacher?

The dress Fräulein von K. usually wore was faded and out of fashion. It had certainly seen better days, but it was always clean and hung with dignity on her frail shoulders. She was wan and seemed almost weightless. Her voice was very tenuous, as if it came from far away. Her face wore no expression and we exchanged very few words. Sitting at the piano, I played my garbled scales. I was a very poor piano student. I never exercised. Sitting for hours on a narrow stool for practice, was too much for my turbulent spirits.

Fräulein von K. had a strange ailment. One of her eyes was always flaming red and seemed ready to roll out of its socket. Now and again a tepid tear would land on my knuckles, as my fingers did not move nimbly enough on the yellowing ivory keys of the old piano, which produced a sort of discordant lament under the torture of my solfeggio.

Our living room had a covered balcony, which jutted like a medieval turret out from the corner. It commanded a very useful view over the crossroads on which our massive apartment building stood.

This vantage point meant that my sister could dawdle about the house as late as possible in the morning, since she could look out for her friend who lived about three hundred yards down the road and came to fetch her on their way to school. This respite gave her just a few minutes to gulp down her breakfast and finish dressing on the stairs before she would meet her schoolmate under the doorway.

The balcony was our favourite haunt. It was somewhat secluded from the rest of the house and gave us ample opportunity to observe what was going on in the neighbourhood. It was not long before our attention was drawn by a well-dressed young man who trained his dog on a wide grassy patch at the back of the large hotel on the main thoroughfare, some distance from our building.

We soon decided we would go and watch the dog's antics. Standing at the edge of the small field, we would marvel as the beautiful wolfhound jumped higher and higher every day over a stick held at arm's length by his master. We soon became friends with the young man and one day, moved by our assiduity and unconcealed admiration for his dog's progress, he went as far as to promise us that when Fritz, for that was the name of his champion, had found a worthy mate, he would present us with one of his puppies. We were overjoyed at the idea of owning a dog all of our own.

The urge to possess a pet animal, common to so many children, is, I believe, a reaction to their parents' emotional and undisputed power of authority over their every independent impulse. They, in their turn, feel the necessity to extend their love and authority over some dependent creature. We had long forgotten the young man's promise, when he appeared at our door, one day, nestling a small bundle under his arm. The soft muzzle of a brown puppy emerged from the folds of an old blanket. We could not hide our happiness and thanked him profusely.

My sister decided we would call the little dog Jazz. I thought the name was a little affected. We soon realised it was not an easy job to cope with a wolfhound in a third-floor flat full of fragile porcelain objects and delicate antique rugs. The puppy's excretions soiled the entire flat and could not always be located and neutralised in good time.

As soon as he grew up his favourite game was to rush at full speed under the flimsy legs of the frail tables bearing our highly prized Chinese vases. Our elders almost collapsed with heart seizure and we trembled lest they took the dog away from us. What was worse, our dear pet gave off a very unsavoury smell. We washed him often with soap and water, but he would catch cold every time. We were then advised to use talcum and he was so heavily powdered that every time he moved about, our whole apartment appeared to have been hit by a mock snowstorm.

The puppy was growing into a sizeable dog whose shows of affection for us were somewhat overpowering. He soon took up most of our spare time. We played around with him to such an extent, that our homework was often neglected. In the end he was strong enough to be put through all the tricks we wanted him to learn. We took him to the little field down the road and taught him to bring back the stick or stone we threw further every time and finally to jump over a stick. He had grown into a beautiful wolfhound with muscles rippling under his shining coat. We paraded him on the leash through the streets to show him off to our friends. We were very proud of him.

Jazz, however, was becoming very independent and often ran away if the street door had been left open by accident. He would roam around in the neighbourhood and come back after a short while. One day he did not return from his usual escapade. Night came and he had not come home. We were fraught with despair. In addition to the hurt we felt at his disappearance, we were heartbroken by his infidelity, by his lack of gratitude for all our love and care. And then a terrible thought assailed us. Had he been run over and killed under a tramway or a carriage?

Eight days went by, eight sorrowful days, and then one morning as the sheep flocked under our windows we heard the unmistakable bark of our dog coming from afar, almost from the bottom of the long uphill road which ended on our street. We ran to the window. He could not be seen in the midst of all the sheep. Then all of a sudden he jumped out of the surging mass and bounded towards our door.

We hardly had time to open the door before he jumped into our arms. He seemed mad with excitement. His bark was alternatively joyfully and plaintive as if to express how unhappy he had been to be away from us. He smelled strongly of sheep and there was caked mud on his paws and under his belly. We concluded that he had been taken away to the hills by the shepherds who wanted him to guard their flocks.

Some time after this distressing episode, Jazz did not burst into our bedroom in the morning, to give us a lick on the face as usual. We went to look for him and found him panting on his mattress near the kitchen. He was in agony and looked at us with imploring eyes. We did not know how we could help him. He had probably eaten one of the poisoned meatballs strewn all over the streets by the municipal dogcatchers to do away with as many as possible of the stray dogs that had become a menace. Jazz was breathing raucously and moaning almost inaudibly. It did not last long and soon his chest ceased to heave, his eyes became glassy and his whole body stiffened. He was dead and we were dumbfounded with sorrow. We had lost our friend and constant companion.

As we looked at his poor corpse a disturbing thought entered our minds. How and where could we bury our beloved pet? Dead animals were not much bothered with in the East, and we did not want him to be carried away and thrown on a heap of garbage at the mercy of scavenging birds that would have torn his poor body to pieces. The faithful Albanian, my uncles bodyguard, came to our help. In the quiet of the night, he carried poor Jazz wrapped in a blanket and buried him in the corner of the grass patch on which he had romped joyfully with us, so often. His death left a great void in our daily life and we no longer hurried back from school in the afternoons. My sister and I made a great decision. We would never own a dog again. There was too much sadness in seeing him die.

The European part of the city, the so-called European quarter, was mainly inhabited by the ethnic minorities, Greeks, Armenians and Jews, as well as by many foreigners who despite living in Turkey for a long time had retained their original nationality. The ethnic minorities as a rule enjoyed Turkish nationality. In the better part of the residential quarters there were also a number of well-to-do families of Muslim Turks, who had chosen to live there. The total population of Constantinople did not exceed eight hundred thousand souls at the end of the 1914–18 World War. Two-thirds were ethnic minorities and foreigners and the other third, the real owners, were Muslim Turks who lived mainly on the opposite bank of the European quarters, in Istanbul. Foreigners and ethnic minorities had always been present in the city since the time of Byzantium and had remained there after its conquest by the Turks in 1453. There were Greeks, Armenians, as well as some Jews and a medley of Slavs, Albanians, Syrians and Persians who plied their different trades and activities in the "polis". The bulk of the Jewish population had settled there only at the end of the fifteenth century when they were cast out of Spain by the Inquisition and made welcome in Turkey under Sultan Bayazid II.

Genoese and Venetian traders had settled on the European shore of the city as early as the twelfth century and left evident signs of their passage in the names of the port environments and in the nautical terms which refer to sailing ships. The tower, which was built by the Genoese in the European quarters and commands views of the town and the whole seascape, is called the Galata Tower, while the bridge connecting the two parts of the city is known as the Galata Bridge. The port on the European side is also called Galata: *la calata del porto* means "the port area" in Italian. *Issa* and *poggi* are commands to pull-up or lower the sail from *issa* and *poggia* in Italian. *Varda* is the warning cry of the coachman, warning passers-by to stand aside, or is shouted by the heavy-laden porters wending their way through the crowd. The word comes from the Italian for "Look out!", *guarda*! *Alabanda* means capsizing, from the Italian expression *dare di banda*. *Tersane* from the Italian *darsena* is where boats are careened and repaired. Another word of Italian origin, *dalavera*, is used extensively in common parlance to signify a shady business transaction, or something mysterious, somewhat dishonest. The origin is probably a bookkeeping term used by the Lombards, *dare e avere*. Bookkeeping to the simple mind is always a somewhat mystifying subject.

As steam navigation took over, the maritime terms assumed an English aspect. *Tornistan* came from "turn astern". Most steamships in Turkey were built in Liverpool or Glasgow and on the telegraph dial on the captain's bridge the terms were in English. *Firok* came from "fire up", while *paydos*, "paid off", also referred to the end of a temporary job. These terms may since have been replaced in modern Turkish. I doubt however that they have completely disappeared. The language of the people has very deep roots.

Chapter Two

The autochthonous population of minority ethnic groups and native-born foreigners who were mainly concerned with commerce were disparagingly branded by the outside world as Levantines. This unflattering definition, used with great gusto by slipshod novel writers and by such persons who are always ready to criticise other people's actions, regardless of their own, must be finally cleared of prejudice. It is also inconceivable to a logical mind that a centuries-old commercial centre like Constantinople, the link for all business transacted between East and West, should be characterised by dishonest dealings. I wish at this stage to throw some light on commercial behaviour in Turkey in my day, as well as in the past as explained to me by my elders.

Among all those who transacted business or plied a trade, from street vendors to important merchants, from day labourers to bankers, the given word was a sacred obligation and could not be broken. There were hardly any written agreements and few receipts and promissory notes. A dishonest merchant or tradesman who did not keep his word was totally disqualified, lost his credit and would find it virtually impossible to do business any more. He had generally to emigrate and try to make a living elsewhere.

The established custom of bargaining, typical of all sales transactions in the East, does not imply the intention on the part of the seller to obtain an illicit gain. Bargaining is a game and if it does not take place the vendor feels he has been defrauded of his pastime. Any buyer is supposed to be able to stand his own ground, according to Oriental mentality. Even a foreigner. Important transactions between responsible merchants hardly contemplated the need for bargaining. Price limits were known and after a light skirmish the deal was concluded. No signatures were needed. It was sealed with a handshake.

Constantinople, which spread over the low hills and wide plateaus around the half-moon of the Golden Horn, offered magnificent views from many of its vantage points. Turning into one of the side streets, which converged like a cobweb on the main thoroughfare and shopping centre of Pera, the European quarter, one would be confronted with a magnificent panorama. It might be the Golden Horn, shimmering like a silver mirror in the early morning or turning into molten gold at sunset. Or else one's eyes would roam over the boundless expanse of the Sea of Marmara, criss-crossed by vessels of all kinds, like little toys in the distance. On a clear day with a windswept sky one could make out, almost merging with the horizon, the cluster of the pine-covered Princes' Islands. At night, from the residential quarters, the Bosphorus, the mythical furrow carved by the legendary steer that severed the continents, would appear in all its beauty, flowing in a ripple of contrasting currents towards the Black Sea.

Shining in the splendour of the sun, like pearls in a royal diadem, the white-painted ancestral dwellings of the nobility, the stately *yali*, hard by the water as if emerging from its depths, lined the banks of the majestic stream. Dotting the background of the luxuriant vegetation covering the low hillsides framing the dark blue waterway, red-roofed white cottages peeped here and there, lost in the woods.

The front of the building where we lived overlooked the second main thoroughfare that, starting from the banking and business centre around the port of Galata, ascended slowly through anonymous, middle-class dwellings to reach the well-to-do residential quarter and the better-class hotel area on the flat. This large road finally re-joined the famous Grande Rue de Pera, the most elegant artery of the European quarter, at a busy crossing. Lined with well-stocked fashionable stores and exclusive pastry shops, and passing in front of the Catholic church of St Antoine, it ended its course at Tünel

Square, where one of the first two-wagon underground railways of its time plied to and fro down to Galata.

Crossing the Golden Horn on the Galata Bridge, which links the European quarters with the Turkish part of the city, one would enter a completely different world. Istanbul in a large semicircle around the Golden Horn, reached the apex of its outer rim and turned towards the Sea of Marmara at Seraglio Point. Surging magnificently above a mass of large buildings and wooden constructions covering the hillside, imposing mosques crowned the landscape all along the skyline.

The residential districts of the Turkish population presented distinct characteristics which set them apart from the European quarters. Few passers-by wandered up the steep, haphazardly cobbled, tortuous streets that led into the maze of non-descript small houses. Here and there a capacious, three-storey, lovely wooden building indicated the abode of some more important family. Wooden shutters pierced with small apertures, *musharabieh* as they were called, protected the intimacy of the householder who could look out into the street but remain invisible to the inquisitive eye. Turkish women would not usually loiter on the doorstep. The narrow streets were the playground of cheeky barefoot urchins who aped the imprudent passer-by, or attached themselves, in swarms, to the back of the occasional rickety carriage which ventured into this hidden world pulled by a lean-looking horse.

Emerging from the labyrinth of the winding streets one would sometimes come across an open, grass-covered space surrounded by cypress trees. A *türbeh*, or covered kiosk protecting the marble tomb of some venerated saintly person, would mark the centre or occupy the corner of the area. Often, there would be a fountain of clear water running from the side of the kiosk. A laudatory inscription on a marble slab would mention the name of the good Sultan who had brought this clear water to the thirsty. There would certainly be a booth serving tea or coffee to customers who would sit on narrow straw-covered stools at little tables under the trees. Sometimes, in a corner, there would be an old man smoking his bubbling *narguileh*,[5] pervading the air with a sweet opiate perfume, looking very wise and completely detached from any earthly problem. His unfocused gaze seemed to look into eternity.

Over the massed dwellings on the hillside, the Topkapi Palace towered in all its splendour, surrounded by high cypress trees. From its terraced gardens one overlooked the Old Walls of Byzantium, the Hippodrome and the Egyptian Obelisk.

The commercial activity of Istanbul had grown up mainly on the right of the bridge where a seemingly endless expanse of winding streets ascended from the waterside up to the crest of the hills. Tradesmen offering the same kind of goods or artisans practising the same handicraft were clustered

---

[5] *Narguileh*: tobacco water-pipe

together in areas named after the goods sold or the article manufactured. One encountered an incredible variety of merchandise in this vast emporium, where trades and handicrafts had been exercised on the same spot since Byzantium was founded and where shops, booths, warehouses and workshops still showed the marks of their antiquity on their weathered brick facades.

Standing out from the shops clustered around its massive structure like a colony of ants, the immense, high-vaulted building of the Grand Bazaar extended its offshoots in every direction. The strident voices of the criers merged in a deafening chorus with the guttural warning shouts of the sweating porters, who pushed their way into the tumultuous crowd milling through the bazaar, at all times of the day, buying and bargaining or just loitering wide-eyed at the wealth of goods offered for sale.

On the wide main road, which started at the head of the bridge, large stores, in the European style, gave a more modern aspect to the old city. The upper part, however, was crowded with the usual type of small shops. Here and there massive old buildings, the so-called *hans*[6], dominated the surroundings. These extensive compounds, which sometimes had entrances on two or three side streets, housed the opulent warehouses of the largest merchants.

---

[6] A *han* fulfilled the functions of a caravanserai and accommodated visiting caravans, namely merchants who travel together for greater protection.

All along the docksides of the Golden Horn, at the base of the effervescent business quarters, heavy, wide-flanked Black Sea mahones were usually moored alongside one another, in considerable numbers. These large sailing barges supplied the food market with fish, fruit and vegetables from the Turkish provinces on the Black Sea.

The food market extended for hundred of yards along the waterside and adjoined an endless series of derelict low wooden warehouses, where all sorts of commodities were stored. The invigorating smell of tobacco leaves laid out to dry under the corrugated iron roofs and the pungent fragrance of outlandish spices mingled with the overpowering stink of raw hides stocked in the vicinity as we rowed lazily towards the outlet of a small river, almost at the end of the right bank, at the head of the bay. Its winding course ran through reed-lined banks along lush meadows covered with buttercups or red poppies, according to the season.

On the heights, at the bottom of the Golden Horn, large clusters of green cypresses shaded an age-old cemetery. Slanting marble slabs scattered at random, surmounted by a carved turban or by the semblance of a tasselled fez, stood up from the thick grass. Here and there a *turbeh* containing one or more tombs sheltered the eternal peace of some high official or venerable person who had enjoyed a sultan's favour. Towards the end of the day, this refuge of the dead became alive with a motley crowd of people, young and old, who picnicked among the tombs, waiting for the sun to set. At times, a domestic sheep, brought along by his master, would munch a long bladed tuft of grass, in some forgotten corner.

The last oblique rays of the setting sun, sharply illuminating the hillside, would enliven the colours of the Turkish women's ample garments and play upon the shining turret-shaped, brass containers carried by the lemonade and water vendors who moved incessantly among the sitting crowd of onlookers. In a tinkle of tiny bells and silver coins hanging from their long-spouted urns, they would dispense ice-cold lemonade or crystal-clear water, tilting their body so as to project a jet of liquid in a perfectly aimed parabola into a glass held in their hand.

As the sun slowly settled towards the West, a sudden hush would fall upon the crowd. The majestic domes and the slender minarets would be silhouetted against the flaming sky in an unforgettable vision and an eerie white light, which skimmed the top of the dark cypresses, would descend upon the marble tombs. Like a sea of flame, the water of the bay would slowly lose its brilliance and then, all of a sudden, the enchantment would die, leaving a twilight of veiled shadows and muffled voices. Here and there the first lights of the night would pinpoint the darkness.

A very mixed crowd moved incessantly through the streets of Istanbul, the oldest part of the city and the centre of commercial activities and handicrafts of all kinds. Mostly of Oriental origin, the people presented an exhaustive array of the various races.

Ambling along with a lost expression on their face and keeping to the middle of the road, Anatolian peasants were easy to recognise, in their characteristic costume. They were dressed in *shalvar*, wide pantaloons fastened around the ankles and hanging at the back in a kind of a sagging appendage. Over a collarless, boldly striped shirt, they wore a short broadcloth waistcoat with a wide white or red woollen sash slung in various folds around their waist. The sash contained their most prized possessions. A purse for their hard-earned coins, a tobacco box and cigarette paper, a handy knife and sometimes a thick onion-shaped, silver watch, of which they were inordinately proud. Older peasants would wear a fez, over which a modest turban indicated that they did not count themselves as very high up in the social scale of turban wearers. In addition, their ordinary clothing would be protected by a wide, cloth overall without buttons.

Country people walked in thick leather, cloglike, low-heeled slippers, with an upturned point or sheepskin soles bound around their legs crosswise with narrow strips of the same material. Kurds and Albanians differed very little from one another in their way of dressing but there were some details, above all their completely different features, which made them easily set apart.

Persians were quite numerous within the particular traffic centres in which they plied their own specialised trades. An astrakhan calotte and a dark grey cotton caftan helped in their identification. Levantines of various walks of life dressed according to their social position, a scattering of foreign tourists, policemen, soldiers, beggars and hawkers of all kinds milled along the shop-lined, winding streets or in the labyrinth of the Grand Bazaar.

Amid the masculine crowd one would also come across some Turkish women on a shopping errand. Swathed in their ample dress, the *çarşaf*, they would glide among the noisy multitude. The shapeless cotton or silk garment, which hid their figure to the impious eye, consisted in a wide cape and hood over an ample skirt which fell down to their feet. At face level a small aperture in the hood and covered with a veil offered these ladies the opportunity of throwing a furtive look around. The veil did not always consist of the same almost opaque, drab material. Beautiful women seemed willing to allow their suggestive, khol-circled eyes to be fugitively admired through the tracery of a tenuous curtain of featherweight tulle.

In the vicinity of the dockside on the Golden Horn where their capacious Black Sea mahones were moored, the Laz sailors walked two by two. These sturdy boatmen, linked together by their little fingers, would strut in the middle of the road as if it belonged to them, looking boldly at everyone and passing remarks in their incomprehensible dialect. The Laz people lived on the shores of the Black Sea around Trebizond, the Byzantine colony founded by Basil Comnenus in 1204. Their origin is somewhat of a mystery. Their light complexions, fair hair and blue eyes are strikingly different to the usual features of the surrounding population of Asia Minor. These Laz mariners looked very elegant in their black costumes with tight hose-like trousers and closely fitting double-sleeved jerkins on which half of each sleeve was slashed lengthwise and hung behind their back. The silver buttons on their jerkins and the soft leather boots they wore on their feet gave them a particularly smart appearance. A black, silver-bordered, cloth scarf was wound around their head, leaving one of the ends hanging behind the neck. Self-confident and always ready for a fray, they would use their knives without any qualms. If one left them alone, however, and did not react to their boisterous conduct, they would not interfere with the peaceful citizens. In matters of trade they were utterly honest and reliable. Once given, they kept their word and would meet friendliness with warmth and loyalty. They were generally liked and excused for their bravado.

Walking through the European quarters across the bridge the appearance of the people one encountered was very different. Except for the Kurdish porters on the dockside of Galata, the uniformed policemen, the tram drivers, coachmen, bootblacks and the itinerant vendors in the morning, one could easily imagine oneself in any of the more up-to-date large port towns on the Latin shores of the Mediterranean. People walking about the streets were in general Levantines or foreigners. In the fashionable stores on the main street and even in the smaller shops, the goods displayed were mostly imported from Europe or copied locally on Paris or London models. A passing foreigner would have looked in vain for the Oriental atmosphere he would expect. The inhabitants of that part of the city regarded themselves as living in Europe, which was partly true, geographically.

In the streets and shops one heard French or Greek spoken by passers-by and by customers and shop assistants. Turkish, as spoken by a large majority of foreigners born in Turkey and even by the ethnic minorities, was really not up to standard. There were, of course, among the Ottoman subjects of non-Turkish origin, a number of persons who aspired to government office and went through Turkish high schools and universities. As a matter of fact, the Turkish language as it was spoken, especially at that time, with a considerable proportion of Arabic and Persian words, lent itself beautifully to the art of literary and polite conversation.

Foreigners who had lived in Constantinople for generations retained their original nationality and were not considered Ottoman subjects, in spite of the fact they had been born in Turkey. This state of things was due to an agreement called the Treaty of Capitulations. It had been granted by Sultan Süleyman the Magnificent to King Francis I of France in 1536 as a reparation for the murder of a French friar at the hands of mob of Muslim fanatics.

This treaty was originally only in favour of French subjects, but it was later extended to all foreign nationals in Turkey. The privilege granted to foreigners allowed them a status of extraterritoriality which made them independent from Turkish law. Their homes were considered as a part of the territory of the nation to which they belonged. Since they were born in their own houses they were deemed to have first seen the light in their country of origin.

A foreigner's abode was inviolable. If, having infringed Turkish law, he was liable to being arrested, a Turkish policeman could not take him away without an authority granted by his consulate and unless he were accompanied by a consulate official. He would have to be taken to a special prison for foreigners and judged by a so-called mixed tribunal consisting of foreign magistrates. The Treaty of Capitulations was abolished in 1923 as a result of the Lausanne Conference.

Owing to these special circumstances, foreigners in Turkey remained permanently attached to their country of origin, to its particular traditions and culture, and this naturally fostered in them the desire to educate their children accordingly. Various foreign schools were set up in Constantinople for that purpose. French, English, German and Italian could be studied in these establishments with the same curriculum as in the home country. The French had been the first to propagate their system of education through the medium of various orders of priests, Jesuits and Dominicans, as well as by nuns to take care of the female students. This early pre-dominance of French schools explained the prevalence of that language among the ethnic minorities who regarded themselves as primarily European.

At the beginning of the twentieth century English, German and Italian schools were also opened, vying with the French institutes. Foreign schools were also frequented by the children of upper-class Turkish families who lived in the European quarters. In addition to these schools, the various national groups had each their own clubs and associations where they congregated to keep alive the tradition and the way of life of their country. The British played tennis and cricket and organised amateur football games. The Germans met at the Teutonia, a club-cum-gymnasium and bowling alley where they sang patriotic hymns. The French dispensed literary lectures and theatrical performances at the Union Française. They also practised fencing. The Italians did much the same at the Dante Alighieri Institute, although their fencing was somewhat different because their foils had a different hilt.

A large proportion of foreigners were born in Turkey but kept their original nationality as a result of the Treaty of Capitulations. My family enjoyed British nationality because our original family nucleus had been established in Gibraltar, which became part of the British Empire in 1718 following the Treaty of Utrecht. Although I was born in Constantinople from parents who had also been born there, I considered myself a foreigner, a loyal subject of His British Majesty, and duly frequented the English High School for Boys as soon as this institute was reopened after the 1914–18 War. My intent, and that of my parents, was that I should gain command of the English language and also benefit from a British education, such as being taught the rules of gentlemanly behaviour, a respect for law and tradition, which as a Jew was already familiar to me, and, above all, a sense of fair play. This particular respect for equity, albeit sometimes laid aside by the British for the sake of their country, does all the same torment their conscience to the extent of allowing them to admit publicly, and with shame, that wrong has been done.

There were two public gardens in the European district. One of them was well kept, quite spacious but rather far away, while the other, very near to my home, adjoined the large hotel building that loomed opposite our windows. The Pera Palace was the most important establishment of its kind in Constantinople. It was world-famed for first-class service and comfort on European standards and its massive bulk looked very much like one of the monumental hotels on the Ring in Vienna. In its large central ballroom, surmounted by a glass cupola, the smart upper set periodically organised brilliant charity balls in aid of one or other of the many welfare institutions in the city.

The small garden where I usually spent my afternoons of leisure, once I had been definitively freed from the yoke of a governess, was completely unadorned in terms of flowers and trees. Its main attraction was a Navy brass band, which lavished sonorous concerts on the public every day from four to six. It played lively marches, operetta music and well-known opera overtures under the directorship of a fierce-looking, black-moustachioed naval officer, who wielded his baton like a cavalry sabre. The white bandstand stood in the very centre of the garden area, which was covered with sand and pebbles and afforded an easy walking surface.

There was also another quite important reason that made this garden interesting to the teenage generation of both sexes living in the neighbourhood. It was an authorised spot where boys and girls could meet each other without giving rise to gossip. Walking leisurely around the bandstand, boys in one direction and girls in the other, lovelorn youngsters had the opportunity of exchanging amorous glances with their secret sweethearts. If they did not meet on the first roundabout, he or she simply reversed direction. After a period of silent counting, boy and girl would greet each other timidly. The girls would bow their head bashfully and young males would lift their straw hats with studied nonchalance. Straw hats were the fashion then and worn even by youngsters still in breeches. Finally one of them would muster up enough courage to stop and talk. It was not done to indulge in long conversations. Although consumed with love, it was not done to confess one's passion.

In the end, after an endless series of circles around the bandstand we would get tired of this unmanly mawkishness. We would retire to the back of the garden which overlooked a disused cemetery. There was always open warfare between us and the small fry of the gypsies encamped among the fallen tombstones. The battle would start with a contest of insults. Bland on our part, blasphemous from the opposite side. We could never match the vocabulary of the street boys. Bad language among well-bred youngsters was still in its infancy. A hot skirmish with an exchange of stone missiles would follow these preliminaries and there again we would draw a short straw. In the end we would retire home with a black eye and a burst straw hat. The afternoon promenade would be resumed the next day, cleaned up and looking our best, and quite often sporting a new boater.

There was always a soft breeze playing around the street corners, blowing from the Bosphorus or the Sea of Marmara. It wafted the characteristic scents of the teeming city. In the daytime the pervading aroma of ground coffee would overwhelm the others. Robust, bare-armed assistants would work beside the ubiquitous coffee booths, lifting their heavy pestles over the wide-brimmed mortars filled with roasted beans and as the dark mass was pulverised the inebriating fragrance would explode into the air.

Well before midday *şiş kebab* would be roasting outside restaurant doors all over the business and shopping area. Slung over a vertical spit, revolving in an open, upright oven lined with glowing charcoal, succulent slices of mutton, seasoned with titillating spices, would make one's mouth water, as the surface of the thick roll of meat formed a dark savoury crust. This was soon joined by another scent. As the baker's assistant trotted on his horse through the busy streets, astride two large panniers of freshly baked loaves of crusty bread, the unmistakable wholesome perfume would linger in his wake.

At times, however, a whiff of less pleasant odours would shock one's sense of smell for a while. The rickety garbage cart would make its way through the throng, losing some of its contents here and there. The kerosene vendor would add to the unpleasant smells as he pushed his handcart over the uneven road surface, spilling some of the liquid from the open tin cans. The dried codfish and anchovy vendor would fill the atmosphere with an overpowering stink as the anchovies wallowed in the filthy brine of the oozing barrel. However, these mixed odours would quickly blow away. There was always a fresh breeze from the Bosphorus to air the streets of this wonderful city.

Having left the outskirts of the town behind it did not take long to reach the open countryside. Few houses were scattered along the roads that led to the suburbs. There were green meadows all around, covered with narcissi, daisies and buttercups or poppies, as the season changed. The verges were lined with sweet-smelling time-trees or tall cypresses. In the gardens around the country houses bloomed heady scented jasmine and honeysuckle. Roses gave off a delicate, almost evanescent odour and carnations radiated an overpowering, savage, musky scent.

The coastline was never far away. From the highest part of the European quarter tumbling roads descended sharply towards the shores of the Bosphorus. On the other side of the bridge, from Istanbul, it was easy to reach the shoreline of the Sea of Marmara. Nearly all the way along the waterside one came across bathing establishments. These low, wooden cabins, built on stilts and standing side by side to form a square above a limited expanse of water, were joined to the mainland by a long footbridge which branched off at its extremity, separating two identical blocks. The bathing areas for men and women were duly set apart to protect the ladies' pudency.

Up to the age of four, my mother would take me with her when she went swimming. A concert of strident female screams would rend one's ears on approaching the ladies' compound. There was a narrow platform running all along the front of the cabins with a ladder on opposite corners, which served to climb down into the sea. It stood about a yard and a half above sea level. Most women would go into the water a rung at a time, very carefully, testing the temperature of the water lest it should be too cold for their liking. They would hardly keep silent when dipping a foot tentatively into the sea-water. Others, younger and daring, would jump feet first from the platform, pinching their nose with two fingers and emitting a piercing scream at the same time.

Women's costumes were exceedingly proper and never offended decency, covering the ladies almost up to the neck and down to the knees. Some very prudish Turkish woman would even go into the water in a long, canvas-coloured linen frock. In those times it was also the rule for men to wear striped costumes in black and white or navy blue, which left only their arms and legs bare. Men could swim out from the bathing compounds into the open sea. This rule also applied to the European women, but it was absolutely forbidden to Muslim Turkish women to leave the precincts of the bath house and mix with the men.

I learned how to swim when my mother abandoned me one day clinging to the stout rope which traversed the narrow side of the inside pool and served to support non-swimmers. She waited for me some four or five yards away at the base of the ladder urging me to join her. In my despair, I suddenly mustered enough courage to take the plunge and, half in, half out, managed to swim the short distance, spluttering and half-drowned. After this daring performance I convinced myself I was a good swimmer and lost my fear of the water.

On approaching these bath houses a smell of rotting wood and the muddy shallows would meet one's nostrils. So many years have gone by and yet the memory of this particular smell haunts me at times and takes me back to the happy period of my infancy. Deeply embedded in the subconscious, long-forgotten sensations come awake suddenly with incredible clarity. When, in the country, of a summer evening, the song of the cricket comes to my ear, relentless in the silence of the setting day, I feel a deep melancholy. I still perceive, alive and awe-inspiring, the clinging sentiment of fear which weakened my knees, when in my early childhood I used to run back home at sunset, all alone, through silent meadows and whispering thickets, followed at every pace by the chirp of the cricket whose rhythm matched my heartbeats.

As I look back to the carefree days of my childhood, I remember my Uncle Eugene with particular tenderness. Tall, spare and distinguished, he personified the best aspect of the pre-1914–18 War generation of German intellectuals. He was gentle and kind and took to heart our orphaned condition. Every Sunday morning he would come to fetch us, my sister and I, and take us for long walks into the country or to the museums across the bridge in Istanbul. At midday before going back home we would visit a German *biergarten* and there, sitting like grown-ups at a table in the garden, we would be treated to exquisite toasted *saltzstangen* with butter and cheese and a very small beer. I still remember the delectable taste, which makes my mouth water.

Uncle Eugene was a born educator. He had a son and daughter from his first wife, but they were already married and lived in Germany. His second marriage with my mother's elder sister had remained barren. He had been unhappy with his first wife, who had deceived him sordidly and had even managed to estrange him from his children. I think he was bestowing upon us all the love he had been unable to give to his own son and daughter. I learned much from my uncle. Up to this day I dare not leave a morsel of food on my plate even when my appetite has gone. When lunching at his table, he urged us never to leave a grain of rice. This was the rule.

As I grew up, this good uncle showed particular intuition of my adolescent wishes and tried to fulfil them if they were reasonable. In a closet, at the very end of the entrance hall of his apartment, he had kept a Flobert gun, which had belonged to his son. This gun had been the object of my fondest desires ever since I had set eyes on it as a child. Uncle Eugene had promised I would have it when I was fifteen. The day finally arrived and it was mine. Soon afterwards I shot at a sparrow and killed it. I was so upset at having taken the poor little bird's life that I never shot again at any animal. Instead I built myself a wooden box with a hole at the top through which I could take aim at the wick and flame of a candle. I got so good at it that I could snuff the candle with my first shot. It made me very proud.

Uncle Eugene's house was full of interesting things. A long-barrelled Bedouin gun, its stock mosaicked with mother-of-pearl, and a curved scimitar in a silver sheath strewn with semi-precious stones hung crosswise on the drawing-room wall. A series of beautiful pipes with amber mouthpieces and *meerschaum* bowls carved to represent a variety of subjects, like a full-bearded, turbaned Turk's head or the lithe torso and sculptural breasts of a naiad, were displayed in a glass case, duly protected against careless fingers. In a break-front, angled rosewood cabinet, two delicate Meissen porcelain coffee cups, moulded and coloured in the shape of an apple and a luscious strawberry, rested on saucers that perfectly imitated mulberry leaves. A miniature silver state carriage in seventeenth-century style, as well as tiny models of chairs and settees of the same period were on show on another shelf of the graceful small cabinet.

Amid all these curios was a thick album of photographs, so cumbersome and heavy it could only be consulted when resting on the small table on which it stood. The cover was in crimson velvet embossed with large silver fleurons and it had a gold nielloed silver clasp with a keyhole. The key was missing and it opened easily. Looking at the photographs was a novel experience. The very characters we had read so much about in our teenage literature – Dickens, Thackeray, Madame de Sevigné and later, Balzac – seemed to be looking at us from these pictures. Bearded gentlemen and wasp-waisted ladies in frilled dresses, generously proportioned both in front and behind, tail-coated beaux sitting stiffly with their top hats on their knees, children of both sexes with hoops and sticks, wearing sailor suits and wide-brimmed straw hats. Family groups with grandfathers and swaddled infants. There were also many military gentlemen. German officers with pointed or plumed helmets, or square-topped uhlan headpieces.

There was also a large photograph of the castle of Schaumburg-Lippe where Uncle Eugene's sister acted as a lady-in-waiting to the princess. In another smaller photo, Uncle Eugene, dressed as a student with a peculiar high-peaked, brimless, cylindrical, silver striped cap, a sash across his shoulders, high knee boots and a sword, was sitting with other students at a table covered with strangely shaped gigantic beer mugs. We had some difficulty in recognising him in a mandarin's costume. The photograph was dated Tianjin, 1896.

After careful scrutiny we also discovered him in a Turkish fireman's uniform. That was certainly an interesting and useful disclosure and we badgered the poor man until he confessed that one of his best friends was an Hungarian major, the Commander-in-Chief of all the fire brigades in Constantinople, who held the exalted rank of Pasha. It did not take us long to convince him to take us to the Firemen's Barracks. We were soaring on air with excitement when we were allowed to get a close look at the huge, red-painted horse-drawn carriages with their shiny brass tanks, the bell, the long ladders, thick ropes and strange hand-tools. In the end, as if by magic, I found myself sitting in the driver's seat with a fireman's helmet coming down to my chin and a hatchet in my hand. My heart was beating very rapidly.

The City Fire Brigade was not large enough to cope on its own with the calamity of frequent, extensive fires. However, long before the Fire Brigade had been set up along European lines, every quarter of the city had had a company of so-called voluntary firemen. These groups were generally manned by the worst elements of their neighbourhood, would rush to the scene of the fire with the speed of lightning. On the Galata Tower in the European part of the city and on another tower, which looked over the opposite bank of the Golden Horn, in Istanbul, there were day and night watchmen, also rather unsavoury characters, who as soon as a fire was located, had to run through the city in order to alert the voluntary firemen in every district. I take it they also alerted the regular Fire Brigade, since their permanence on the watch towers must have been authorised by the local authorities. Muscular and swift as the wind, they ran on high-heeled shoes, which always seemed too small for their feet. They wore a red coat over narrow black trousers and carried a short black ebony stick with a gilt-tipped lance. This was a very smart accessory, which I would have liked to possess. At the watchmen's call the irregular firemen would run all over the whole city in vociferous, hysterical groups, forcing their way through the busy streets. People fearfully stood aside as they passed. Clad in singlets and white calico underpants fastened at the ankle, often bare chested, looking like a horde of devils, they left in their wake the smell of their sour sweat. They carried an old-fashioned hand pump resting on two long poles on their shoulders. Bearers were changed very often in order not to slow the pace of their wild rush. At the scene of the fire they would immediately invade the houses in danger of going up in flames and lay hands on everything that seemed worthy of being carried away, with the intent of reselling it to the owners at a price, or simply to appropriate it at their rightful booty. They were indeed a gang of thieves and often fought among themselves over the booty. Their ridiculous, inadequate pumps, placed anywhere near the fire, would spurt anaemic jets of water on the flames, which only subsided when there was nothing more to burn.

Uncle Eugene was a very knowledgeable person and brought life and excitement to everything we saw on our outings. We learned more about the flowers, the trees and the birds than we did at school, and taking us to museums he would make the inert relics of the past more interesting by telling us their story. We often visited the Janissary Museum, which in those days was located in the Basilica of St Irene, in the Topkapi Palace gardens. I was deeply fascinated by the warlike, compelling expressions of the wax figures, with their menacing moustaches and cruel mouths. I was over-awed by the apparel of strange, fearful weapons they carried. Double-edged hatchets, halberds, damascened-bladed curved daggers, scimitars, and long pistols with silver nielloed stocks. I also admired the strange-shaped monumental turbans and the rich garments adorned with furs and gold braid.

Since those early days I have always nourished a deep interest in the history of these cruel men, whose enemies trembled at the mere mention of their name. With the intent of disposing at all times of a body of professional soldiers completely impervious to outside influence, the Janissaries were torn away from their parents, at the age of eight or nine, on the Sultan orders. Assigned to that special purpose, faithful emissaries travelled across the Christian Balkanic provinces and other territories of the Ottoman Empire and led away the most promising youths. After being duly converted to the Islamic faith, they were educated in the arts of war in special colleges within the precincts of the Sultan's Palace. Transformed into professional killers who managed their weapons with the utmost skill, they were the best-trained and most fearsome warriors in the Ottoman army.

The Janissaries enjoyed many privileges after having concluded their military training, but they were subjected to very strict discipline and were generally confined within the limits of their barracks and training grounds. Marriage was forbidden and their only private contact with the outer world were the prostitutes who came to pay them periodical visits in their quarters. The reason behind these restrictions was the constant fear of their master, the Sultan, that they might become involved in complots or treason against him hatched by the enemies who surrounded him at all times. The Janissaries' food was prepared in huge copper cauldrons. These cooking utensils were, for them, a manifestation of attachment and fidelity to the group; they were a sort of symbol of the family and were taken along on their military expeditions. The Head of the Kitchen was called the *Tchorbadji Bashi* (The Master of the Soup) and held a high rank in the hierarchy of the Janissary Corps. As a matter of fact, he was their virtual Commander, a necessary link to substitute the authority of a father over these rough men. When the Janissaries wanted to express their discontent or exact some new privilege from the Sultan, they would beat incessantly on their cauldrons, producing a dull, menacing sound that would fill the whole population with apprehension.

As time went on their tyrannical power became insupportable and they were finally massacred in their barracks in 1826, by the so-called New Army, which had been organised following the European model by order of Sultan Mahmud II, to free the state from these indomitable warriors and also to endow the nation with military power in keeping with modern standards.

Mahmud II, who was known as the Reformer, had been brought up by his uncle Selim III and his favourite concubine, a French noblewoman called Aimée Dubucq de Riverie who, as a fifteen-year-old girl, educated in France, had been taken by Algerian pirates in the Mediterranean on her return to Martinique, where she had been born. Aimée was sent as a gift by the Bey of Algiers to the powerful Sultan Abdul Hamid I who made her the favourite of his harem.

The young Frenchwoman, who was a cousin of Josephine de Beauharnais, Napoleon I's first wife, was very intelligent and during her mandatory period of harem life had acquired a very sound general culture with the help of several enlightened teachers. In particular, she developed a keen sense of politics. Prince Selim, later Selim III, had spied on her in secret and fell madly in love with the young woman. At the death of Abdul Hamid I, Selim III took Aimée as his secret favourite concubine, since he could not publicly grant her the rank of first favourite as a sign of respect for his uncle's memory. Together, Selim III and Aimée took care to educate Seam's orphaned nephew, the future Mahmud II, who grew up with modern principles. Until her death Aimée Dubucq de Riverie exercised a constant, although hidden influence on Turkish policy during the reigns of both Selim III and Mahmud II, who regarded her as his foster mother.

As a result of the protection afforded to them by the Sultan's favourite, a number of French artisans who had made their living by serving the Court of Louis XVI emigrated to Constantinople where they found a more favourable outlet for their refined artistic skill than in the newly established French popular republic. The evident influence of French style can be easily recognised in Ottoman art during the first part of the nineteenth century.

I owe a enormous debt of gratefulness to my Uncle Eugene for having awakened in me a keen interest in history. As he took me and my sister through the evocative archaeological sites of Istanbul and to the museums he would bring to life the tumultuous magnificent past of the city in which we were so fortunate to live. We were very fond of this uncle who was so close to us and yet not altogether integrated with the rest of the family. A few years after the end of the war he and my aunt left the city to go and live with my maternal uncles in Vienna. Uncle Eugene fell ill. His ailment could not be defined. He gradually faded away, but preserved to the end the dignity of character he had always shown. He had always been very reserved with people and only opened up when he was with us, bestowing his paternal affection. We felt great sadness that he should have to die so far away from us.

I was twelve years old when the war ended. Constantinople was occupied by the Allied Forces. We climbed uphill to watch the fleet coming into the roads from the Sea of Marmara. The warships were awe-inspiring, with ensigns flying, British, French and Italian, and the crews aligned portside. We ran downhill to the port area to meet the sailors who were coming up on leave into the town.

Very soon the Allied uniforms were part of the town panorama. The military went about in noisy groups, making merry like schoolchildren on a picnic. The French were the more boisterous, the British the most drunk, and the Italians the least quarrelsome. The old fashioned cocked hats of the *carabinieri* stood out among the unfamiliar foreign uniforms of the occupying forces.

Shortly after the war ended the French, English and Italian schools were reopened. During the course of the war I had no other alternative but to frequent a German school. Turkish elementary schools, in those days, were quite inadequate for foreigners with their method of teaching based very much on their religion. I learned German quite well but was not very happy in the school's hostile atmosphere. Although a large proportion of students belonged to the ethnic minorities and did not really side with any of the contending powers, the German boys, who were quite numerous in my form, made life quite difficult for me. They knew I was a British subject and did not cease to taunt me. I left that school with no regret when the war was over. The teaching was good but the stiff fanaticism which pervaded the teaching staff grated against my nature. I felt hurt by the disparaging and haughty attitude of the teachers in my regard and their total indifference when I was knocked about by the German boys, so much heavier and older than I was, under the pretence of showing the enemy boy how to box. My annoyance must have been tangible at the compulsory march past, flying the German flag, in front of the Head of the School standing stiffly at attention. These mishaps of my early schooldays would have left no mark and I would have been gratified by the seeds of culture I had imbibed at that stage of my life were it not for the shock and revulsion I felt at Nazi barbarism. Yet, nonetheless, from the depths of the uncontrollable subconscious sometimes my ear will still thrill at the soft, touching words and melody of Heine's unforgettable *Lieder*, which our young music teacher taught us to sing, allowing herself in those rare moments to show her passionate soul, so carefully hidden under her rigid upbringing.

After a short period in a French *lycée*, I finally entered the English High School for Boys in Constantinople. The method of teaching and the particular atmosphere of this school, where the importance of practising sport was almost equal to the attention paid to educational subjects, exercised a marked influence on the development of my personality. Didactic matters were rationally explained. Learning was not an effort, except for mathematics which I found rather irksome. I was deeply interested in the study of history and literature. I learned to understand and admire Shakespeare thanks to a talented teacher who read his plays like an Old Vic professional. He looked very much like Mr Chips.

The post-war period endowed the city with a new kind of life. Allied military missions consisting of brilliant, well-educated officers of the various nations established themselves in the best residential quarters and were soon absorbed by the smart society. Then, in large groups, Russian refugees from Bolshevism poured into the city. The newcomers were for the most part cultured people. They spoke French perfectly and behaved with distinction. The women were generally good-looking and used their makeup with consummate art. The men clearly possessed a thorough knowledge of international Europe. As they declared, they all belonged to the Russian nobility. They were princes, dukes and so forth. These émigrés integrated themselves very easily with the city's well-to-do population and brought about many hitherto unknown novelties.

Night clubs, beauty parlours, ballet dancing academies and fencing clubs were opened in the European quarters, as well as small antique shops where these refugees could display and sell the treasures they had been able to take with them in their flight: pearl-studded icons, beautiful old jewellery, amethyst collars, enamelled silver vessels, and even magnificent Fabergé *objets d'art* and cigarette cases with the Tsar's autograph. There were also medals and orders of merit set with diamonds and enamel.

These scions of nobility endowed the city with exclusive restaurants, smart tea and pastry shops, and they even organised ballet, theatrical shows, operetta performances of a good level. They all seemed to be able to play music and sing professionally. The tidal wave caused by these Russian émigrés had a noticeable influence on the mentality of the people with whom they came into contact. Behaviour in social circles became lax and morality waxed openly free and easy. Dormant instincts became loose and dangerous whirlpools appeared on the surface of the sedate family life of the city. Couples started to divorce, unfaithful matrimonial conduct was no more a secret, and romantic adventures ran the gauntlet. As a matter of fact, the life of the bourgeoisie was very much disturbed and disrupted.

I was fifteen when I came to know Uncle Victor. He was big and tall, a handsome man, with dark hair and a barrel chest. He appeared one evening, as it was getting dark, on the threshold of the little room where I was doing my homework. My mother had often told me about this unmanageable brother of hers, who used to play tricks on poor grandmother. Introducing himself stealthily into the kitchen, he had managed to suck up with a straw all the cream of the *sütlatch*[7] due to be served for dinner, leaving the crinkled surface completely intact. He would also bore a small hole into fresh eggs and empty them of their contents, enjoying his mother's embarrassment when she had to cook an omelette. Too restless to stay under the family roof, he ran away to Vienna when he was barely sixteen. Why to Vienna, I never knew. Very intelligent and industrious, it did not take him long to make a success and he married there, too soon. He had a wife and

---

[7] *Sütlatch*: a kind of milk pudding, creamy, sweet and almost liquid.

daughter who lived with him in Vienna. Now, after many year of absence, he had finally come to see his sisters.

At the door of my cubicle he was looking at me, a hint of sadness in his eyes. He had known my father very well and this was the first time he had seen me after his death.

"Here you are," he said as he came up close and ruffled my hair. "I am told you are a bit of a handful."

He seemed very pleased with this particularity of my character. There and then I felt that he was quite a different kind of uncle. I knew I could talk to him freely. We would be friends and I would confide to him all the mischief I was generally up to.

At home everything was in a flurry. Uncle Victor never stopped for a moment telling his sisters all sorts of spicy stories and laughter filled the normally sedate, muffled atmosphere of the house. There was about his person a hint of sedition, a whiff of revolution. My mother, my aunt and Uncle Victor's four other sisters, who lived in town, crowded around their wayward, beloved brother, who never ceased to make fun of them. The fame enjoyed by Uncle Victor as an impenitent Don Giovanni had preceded him and his sisters were very proud of his amorous conquests. They whispered to each other, recounting his prowess, imagining I could not hear what they said, but I had, long before, engineered many a subterfuge which enabled me, at all times, to listen to what grown-ups talked about in my absence.

The small room in which I was supposed to be always busy attending to my homework was in a very favourable strategic position for my informative purposes. It adjoined the main drawing-room where the ladies of the house received their visiting friends and it was very easy for me to hear what they said, by just leaving the door slightly ajar. If anyone did look into my small room, I was almost invisible crouching behind monstrous piles of schoolbooks. At my desk I was always on the alert. I knew everything about everybody. This curiosity about other people and about all things in general has never abated in my nature, not from a desire to meddle in other people's business, but just from an unquenching thirst for knowledge.

The night of Uncle Victor's arrival was marked by a frightening incident. Past midnight, a Turkish general was assassinated by an Armenian terrorist on the portal of the large hotel opposite our house. The shots echoed sharply in the silence of the night, making us leap out of bed. Barefoot and in underpants, his hairy chest bare to the wind, Uncle Victor was already hanging almost out of the window to watch the unexpected happening. He seemed quite satisfied with this supplement of local atmosphere. In Vienna, such things did not happen every night.

Uncle Victor's arrival had the effect of shaking up our family life. He did it so well and so much that all of a sudden there was no other talk in the household but a journey to Vienna. In a group, all of us.

Behind my guardian and my aunt who regularly, every summer, travelled to Austria, to take the waters at Karlsbad, there now formed a consistent family group. Uncle Victor, my mother, my sister and myself, as well as one of my mother's numerous sisters with her husband and a rather spoilt eight-year-old girl, whom I often had to carry on my shoulders since the dear child had broken a leg which was still encased in plaster.

On a beautiful morning we all crowded into an Orient Express wagon-lit bound for Vienna, taking up almost half of the compartments. The Orient Express was certainly an interesting and unusual sight for me. I did not cease to wonder at the ingenious appliances that made use of every nook and corner to conjure a cosy bedroom out of an ordinary train compartment. These included the small mirrored cupboard with the shining glass water carafe and glasses, the snow-white towels, the reversible washbasin in the corner and the porcelain urinal that fitted perfectly in a cupboard under the washbasin. Reversing the settee that was used in daytime, a soft bed came into view with a small reading lamp at its head. The lamp was hidden under a lid, which snapped like a cigarette case. There was a hook on the wall on which one could hang a watch and a net above the bed for underwear. There were also small closets between two compartments where one could wash and shave. By pulling a bolt on the door the neighbouring passenger could be shut out.

Uncle Victor was very much at ease on the sleeper. He went from one compartment to the other as if he owned the place. The compartment next to us was occupied by a single person travelling alone. A beautiful blonde, a Slav with blue eyes and over-powering charm. She left a trail of heady perfume as she passed. Uncle Victor went all out for the exciting quarry. I was listening to his mesmerising technique with open ears as he was enveloping the blond fairy in the spires of his seduction. I found his method highly educative and I did not miss a word or an inflexion of the voice. The lovely creature looked at him almost in a trance as he passed his arm around her slim waist.

When night fell, uncle Victor said to me, "You sleep on the upper bed. I'll take the lower one."

I was falling asleep. Uncle Victor disappeared into the small toilet. I heard the click of a drawn bolt and a woman's laugh. Much later I woke up with a start as the toilet door was shut and a large shadow slipped back into the lower bed. Uncle Victor had come back from his foray. The day was dawning. A white light filtered past the sides of the black curtain drawn down over the window.

The journey to Belgrade lasted two days. The landscape did not vary much between Bulgaria and Serbia. The peasants' costumes and the uniform of custom officials and frontier guards were different, however. The restaurant car offered a pleasant di-version during the monotony of the journey. Wait-ers balanced food dishes like circus jugglers as the train moved. A medley of languages was spoken at the tables. The menus written in French gave refinement to the good food, which was served in great style.

We arrived at Belgrade in the morning and left the train which proceeded on its journey. We were embarking on a boat that would take us to Vienna on the Danube.

Chapter Three

In front of the station, the waiting carriages drawn by lean horses looked very much like those we had left at the start of our journey. The luggage problem became very acute. There were too many suitcases, small trunks and large round ladies' hat boxes. We had to hire a horse-drawn van and it was decided I would sit perched on top of the mound to escort our possessions. The pile of our personal belongings heaved and caved in, producing a minor earthquake, every time one of the wheels of the van dipped into a hole in the unevenly cobbled road to the river quay.

A large, white paddle-boat was moored at the bank of the river. I shall never forget the enchantment of that voyage on the Danube. On both sides of the waterway wide expanses of yellow cornfields extended into the far distance between clusters of picturesque villages with beautiful baroque church spires. Now and again a small township interrupted the sequence of hamlets. Walking along the road which coasted the river were country people dressed in their traditional peasants' costumes. To me they looked as if they had come out of a geography book. Exciting, colourful travel agency brochures had not yet been invented at this time.

The slow regular motion of the boat favoured an imaginative drowsiness. I had just read Tom Sawyer and Huckleberry Finn's adventures and fancied I was floating with them on a raft on the Great Mississippi River. I could even imagine Mark Twain in person standing at the helm, on the upper deck, which was out of bounds to all passengers.

One night, towards sunset, we arrived in sight of Budapest, whose tall church spires and monumental palaces were silhouetted against the reddening sky. We were coasting beside a small island, covered with gardens full of flowers and blazing with light in the oncoming darkness. Carefree people were jumping into the water with high splashes and joyful cries. On the golden surface of the river slim rowing boats were shooting like arrows under the impulse of eight sparkling oars.

That night there was a ball on the boat deck, which was festively adorned with rows of hanging multicoloured, Japanese paper lanterns. The orchestra played Viennese waltzes while the lady passengers, in décolleté evening dresses, danced in the arms of the smartly uniformed officers or gentlemen of varying ages in more or less up-to-date frock coats.

It was a feast of lights and colours on the dark waters of the Danube, as the boat cut its way into the night.

We arrived in Vienna the next day, in the morning. As we left the quay in a large, high-wheeled coach drawn by a pair of tall, robust horses, I felt I was entering a completely new world compared to the turmoil and clamour of the city I had left behind a few days before.

It was Sunday and early in the morning. Driving through the wide, almost empty streets we only heard the swishing of the rubber-padded wheels and the regular beat of the horses' hooves on the even surface of the pavement. Half asleep as I was, it seemed to me we were driving through a city that had been put to sleep under an enchantment. The massive grey buildings, all alike in style, the few sedate passers-by, the absence of noise and the swing of the carriage held me in a sort of trance. As we arrived at the large hotel on the Ring where we were due to stay for a while, the unusual sight of the doorman standing in front, under the roofed entrance, wearing a long, gold-braided cloak and a feathered cocked hat, added to the strangeness of these new surroundings.

We did not stay long in Vienna that time since my uncle and aunt had to proceed to Karlsbad for their usual cure and we all went with them. Karlsbad was a bright and pleasant resort surrounded by low hills covered with green pine forests. On both banks of the small river that traversed it stood luxurious hotels with flower-adorned balconies and wide terraces, which were brilliantly illuminated in the evening when smart people dined to the sound of gipsy music.

I must admit I did not pass the time very happily in this jewel among the famous health resorts of Mitteleuropa. There was very little to do for a fifteen-year-old youngster who did not take the waters.

We left Karlsbad to go to Bad Gastein, in the Tyrol. The radioactive baths there were very salutary for my guardian and aunt who were continuing to follow their annual health cure. I remember the breathtaking high mountain panorama, a sight that was completely new to me, and a thunderous waterfall right in the middle of the fashionable resort. There was a short, wooden bridge with glass viewing panes for observing the foaming waters breaking on the rocks below. The roar of the cascade sounded in one's ears, all around.

We used to go for long rides into the valley, in large coaches drawn by four hefty horses and often stopped at Hof Gastein for the exquisite Sandtorte. It is shameful I should remember so vividly the taste of that delicacy, while the exciting panorama of the snowy peaks and the deep valleys is somewhat blurred in my memory.

We returned to Vienna and stayed there for a fortnight. I visited beautiful museums and rode on the Great Wheel in the Prater. I was getting used to this new world where everybody seemed to have come out of the same mould, where itinerant vendors did not cry their wares under your window in the morning, where people spoke to one another without gesturing, and unruly crowds did not jostle in the streets as they usually did in the city where I was born.

And then the interlude came to an end. We were going back home. We arrived at Constantinople by train. The Orient Express of the beginning of the journey had now lost its novelty. Climbing up, on the road which, after crossing the bridge, traversed the low, popular quarters of the European district towards its more opulent extension on the higher ground of the city, I was stuck by the decaying aspect of the buildings, the peeling walls, the disorderly mass of dwellings of all kinds and the poorly dressed, tired-looking passers-by, going homewards at the end of the day. What I had seen and left behind was a wealthier world, where the orderly aspect of all things gave the impression of a happier way of living. I felt a sudden sadness, which lingered on until, as the tired horses of our carriage almost came to a halt at the top of the hill, I was overwhelmed by the breathtaking sight of the Golden Horn shimmering like a mirror in the flaming light of the setting sun.

The journey to Europe had been a very interesting experience. I acquired the fame of a great traveller among my friends. It seemed almost as if I had crossed the Sahara Desert, all on my own. They all wanted to know what the outside world was like, the Europe to which we half belonged, geographically, but which was unknown to many of us who only spoke its languages and had studied its history.

No one travelled very much into Anatolia in those days. Our life evolved around the capital and its suburbs, and the rest of the country was almost unknown to us. Journeying inland was considered something of an adventure and Europeans avoided it as much as possible. Merchants travelled there for the necessity of their trade, buying the commodities they needed for export or distributing the goods they imported into the country. All the beauty of Anatolian Turkey, which few of us knew about then, was unexplored territory. Some of the names of its cities were more familiar to us because we had friends or relatives who lived there, but we considered them very much like pioneers on the fringes of civilisation.

Our travels were normally limited to a short train journey to the suburbs on the coast of the Sea of Marmara, mostly to a wide sandy beach called Floria, which was patronised by young and old, indifferent swimmers for the most part, who went there to bask in the sunshine or picnic in the small taverns under the sparse trees on the edge of the beach.

It was more of an adventure and a real voyage to cross the sea on a ferry to the Asiatic coast and board a puffing train, which took one to the scattered suburbs of the hinterland travelling through opulent corn fields and green orchards. There were seven suburbs and the train halted seven times.

There was hardly time to settle in one's seat and enjoy the swing of the swaying carriage when the screeching noise of the brakes announced the arrival at the next station. The small railway stations were all alike. There was a large bronze bell at one end of the platform, which was sounded as the train arrived and energetically struck again when the stationmaster finally lifted his small baton and blew with authority on his whistle.

Travelling on the water, aboard the ferries which shuttled between the Asiatic coast, the Princes' Islands (as they were still called in those days) and the landing pier at the foot of the bridge or on one of those boats which zigzagged between the opposite banks of the Bosphorus, was a usual event and part of many people's daily commute. The large paddle boats, which plied the waters in all kinds of weather, were skilfully handled by experienced captains who contrived impeccable landings against the heaving wooden piers of the various localities they had to service, often in rough seas. By engaging and reversing the steam engines, they manoeuvred as close as possible to the landing stage and then, at precisely the right moment, two stout ropes shot like long serpents out of the vessel's side and were made fast with lightning speed, bringing the ferry to a standstill. It was a great pastime to watch the bustle of the disembarking passengers and the frenzy of those boarding by means of the swaying footboards, which were manhandled and placed between the ferry and the landing stage by the crew and the dockers, all accompanied by loud and coarse imprecations. Women and children, men, young and old, with baskets of all sizes, often trailing behind a sheep or a goat hastened to come on board. Sometimes the sight would assume a thrilling dimension as some belated, panting passenger would take a perilous leap onto the ferry as it was leaving the pier.

In summer we went to the Princes' Islands. They were a favourite summer resort. The four islands, varying in size, had kept their original Byzantine names: Proti, Antigoni, Chalki and Prinkipo. Strangely enough, they were of increasing size, starting from the first. Almost entirely covered with pines, their aromatic scent carried for miles on the sea breeze. The third island, Chalki, was home to the Naval Academy and we could often watch the midshipmen drilling in front of their barracks. When on leave, they embarked on the ferry and their youthfulness and good looks, enhanced by their snow-white uniforms, lent a festive quality to the crossing. Travelling on the Bosphorus was a constant enchantment. One boarded a ferry just for the pleasure of the voyage.

Filing past, hard by the waterside and mirroring themselves in the clear water on both banks of the river, a succession of beautiful, white-painted wooden houses were flanked by older, neglected, palatial mansions with covered trellised balconies and boat sheds under their private landing piers. Here and there a modest, narrow wooden structure would lean half askew against its opulent neighbour. Coasting past these relics of the past brought with it a sense of melancholy.

On the shores of the Bosphorus and up to the entrance of the Black Sea, small independent communities bordered one another. They had their own landing stage where the ferries could moor alongside. From the road which traversed these villages, behind the riverside houses, a mass of small redroofed dwellings fanned upwards, almost to the top of the wooded hillsides. The slow progress of the ferry, between the opposite banks of the wide stream, the dormant atmosphere of the small hamlets, hardly disrupted by the arrival of the ferryboat, and the charm of the landscape brought with it a sense of peace and communion with one's inner self, the relish of a moment of pure happiness.

Such were our usual outings in addition, sometimes, to a carriage drive to a neighbouring forest or to a clear spring at the foot of a nearby hill where the crystalline water tasted of fresh almonds. There was always an open-air, hospitable tavern by the spring. In addition to the traditional *raki*,[8] one could have a bottle of beer, kept ice-cold in a bucket at the bottom of the well. The host also dispensed bread and cheese, olives, tomatoes and cucumbers, as well as both watermelons and sugar melons. One particular treat was small, dried mackerel, roasted

---

[8] *Raki*: a clear alcoholic beverage distilled from a variety of fruits or grains, usually flavoured with herbs and spices, especially aniseed.

over a charcoal fire, *tchiros*, as they were called. The tantalising smell of this dish grew stronger as one neared these shaded, havens of pleasure. Many other delicacies, specially prepared at home for the occasion, would be brought on an excursion of this kind. However, custom dictated that coffee, *lokum* stuffed with pistachio nuts[9] and *mastic*[10] would be provided by the tavern host. There was always a festive Kermesse sense of jollity under the old trees of the tavern gardens.

Merry people from all walks of life congregated on feast-days at such spots, using all kinds of means of transport. Hired horse carriages from town for the bourgeoisie, donkeys, horses or creaking ox-drawn peasant carts for the village people. The fun-loving villagers danced joyfully to the music of pipe and drum, encouraged by the onlookers rhythmic shouts and clapping. The men formed a long chain, their arms around the next dancer's shoulders. Moving forwards and backwards with quick, crosswise, short steps, in perfect unison, they proceeded sideways to the rhythm of the drum, forming a circle which opened up again as soon as it was closed. The first dancer then waved a handkerchief in his raised fist to set the time. Now and again, one of the men would free himself from the group to perform on his own, arms raised, head erect, twisting his body in all directions, without for a moment

---

[9] *Lokum*: Turkish delight.
[10] *Mastic*: a kind of odoriferous tree (resin) gum.

appearing trivial. There was always a spirit of ancestral dignity in these folk dances, The women stood aside, squatting on the grass, muffled in their ample overgarments. On this occasion, some less inhibited teenage girl might lift her veil to show a fresh, youthful face, under the kerchief that carefully hid her head of hair. In the late evening we returned home, tired, dizzy and having eaten too much, but with a profound sense of happiness.

Maybe it is time and distance that, in my memory, portray the years of my youth as a period of serenity. However I think that, in those days, there was always the light of hope in our thoughts and faith in the future. I do not think it is possible nowadays to be so little concerned with the troubles of the world as we were then. I was fourteen years old when I listened to a rudimentary crystal wireless for the first time and as its whispers reached my ears through the earphones I remember noticing that I had gooseflesh and a feeling of sacrilege. I considered such a thing to be outside human possibilities.

I do not think we were any more out of touch in Constantinople than young people in other countries. I rode on a motorcar for the first time when I was twelve. We did not read newspapers. We were not interested in the politics of the nation in which we lived nor in those of the outside world. Yet there were certainly in Turkey at that time, as in all other nations around the world, restless young men who did look ahead, who dreamed of utopistic systems to make all men equal and initiated in the name of freedom, giving birth to more or less secret societies. It has been so forever, and for many reasons: because of an emotional drive fired by a desire for justice, an excess of nationalism, or fatally by the instinct of self-destruction inherent in human nature which compels men to sacrifice their lives for a dangerous cause in which they are convinced they believe. We, guileless youngsters, lived our teenage years thinking about matters that were nearer to us.

We were bound very closely to our family's principles of behaviour, to our ancestral tradition of helping others. Our intuition helped us to sense among our comrades those unfortunate beings who hid their poverty for shame. We were careful not to offend them and offered them our friendship, trying to allay their wish to remain apart, which might bring them finally to sink into moral and material misery as they became resentful and unsociable. We were probably in the right, taking it upon ourselves to help those hounded by adversity instead of delegating that responsibility to the public institutions, which, according to modern ways of thinking have a duty to provide everyone with equal possibilities of earning and a general condition of well-being.

There was a newspaper stand on the main thoroughfare that crossed the European district. It stocked all sorts of foreign magazines. I still remember a vivid picture on the cover of the Italian popular magazine called *La Tribuna Illustrata*, which hung on the front of the booth and was one of the most descriptive. It showed a battle between the French and Annamese troops as the Vietcong were called in those days. Nothing has changed very much since except for the name of the contenders.

There were no comic strips and grown-up youngsters did not impoverish their minds reading them. We loved adventurous tales about voyages and the exploration of still undiscovered far-off countries. They gave free course to our imagination and served very much to satisfy the desire for evasion that is dormant in most young people's mind. At that time youngsters did not normally just leave home when hardly weaned, with a rucksack and a sleeping bag, bound for mysterious, far-away countries, cadging lifts on the way. We read Jules Verne, Fenimore Cooper, Robert Louis Stevenson, Edgar Poe and Joseph Conrad. We also enjoyed the exploits of Buffalo Bill and Nat Pinkerton. I remember reading *Cuore* by the Italian author Edmondo De Amicis in the French translation.[11] I liked his young heroes very much. I felt they were near to me in age and sentiment.

There were many magazines for the young and for those who were young no more and still enjoyed them. In French there was *Le Journal des Voyages* and *Je Sais Tout*. On the cover of this particular monthly there appeared as a sort of illustrated slogan, a dwarfish little man with a monstrous head representing the globe. He pointed his finger to it as

---

[11] *Cuore* (Heart) was published in Italy in 1886. A partial French translation, *Grands coeurs*, by Adrienne Piazzi, appeared in 1892.

1. Victor Eskenazi, İstanbul, 1929.

2. View of the Golden Horn and Topkapı, İstanbul, 1906, year Victor Eskenazi was born.

3. View of the Bosphorous, İstanbul, 1906.

4. The Galata Bridge from Eminönü, İstanbul, 1906.

5. The Galata Bridge as seen from Beyoğlu, İstanbul, 1906.

6. Victor aged seven during his time as a student at the German School, İstanbul, 1913.

7. Victor at the tennis club, İstanbul, 1924.

8. Laure Roditi Eskenazi (back left) on her way to school, İstanbul, 1924.

9. Laure (centre), English School for Girls, İstanbul, 1930.

10. Laure and Victor on their wedding day, Milan, 27 December 1936.

11. Skiing on the Uludağ, 1937.

12. Victor and Laure (standing), Büyükada, 1937.

13. Laure, Isaac Roditi, Victor, Rachel Roditi and unknown, Büyükada, 1937.

14. Victor (left) with his brother-in-law Alfredo Roditi, on the terrace of his in-law's home, Ayazpasha, 1937.

15. Victor and Laure, Manchester, 1940.

16. Captain Eskenazi, Cairo, 1942.

17. Captain Eskenazi in front of the pyramids, Cairo, 1943.

18. Victor and colleagues of British Intelligence, İstanbul, 1944.

19. Victor, İstanbul, 1945.

20. Victor with his children Johnny and Peggy, Milan, 1955.

21. Victor in his gallery in Milan, 1976.

22. Victor and Laure, London, 1982.

Vittorio e John Eskenazi

23. Victor with his son Johnny at their gallery in Milan, 1986.

if to manifest his omniscience. This strange creature always brought to my mind H.G. Wells's *Martians*. Extraterrestrial beings commanded, then as now, a sense of curiosity intermixed with fear. There was no television. No motorcycles for everybody and no discos. We went to the cinema in mixed groups. It was tolerated by parents that girls could go with their girlfriends and other boys on condition there was a brother and sister in the group. Boys and girls behaved with more restraint. There were exceptions of course, which caused great scandal. We flirted all the same, even heavily. There was always a way for a couple to spend a short time together, all alone, thanks to their friends' complicity.

Youngsters tried not to get their girlfriends into trouble and, wherever possible, the girls held fast to their virtue, which they still considered precious enough to keep intact, contrary to what some modern girls now believe. This physical condition is often now seen as an old-fashioned burden to be done away with as soon as a girl reaches high school. In those days, young people could believe in Platonic love without feeling ridiculous. Obscene language was not obligatory and youngsters, who did not exhibit a luxuriant shock of hair or an Afro haircut, lifted their hats with a natural gesture to greet a lady or an older person.

At sixteen I started to dream I wanted to be a doctor. I wished to be like my guardian, to cure the poor and those who suffered, and be loved by everyone. I spoke to him about it, one day. As, almost stuttering with embarrassment, I was explaining the reasons which prompted my choice, I saw his eyes light up with emotion behind his glasses. He put his hand on my shoulder and said to me with great tenderness:

"I am very proud that you should want to dedicate yourself to help your fellow men and that I have been an example to you. To do good is man's first duty in life, but I feel it is right that I should warn you about the hardships of the profession you wish to follow. A doctor's life entails heavy responsibilities. Your time will never be your own. You will have to be ready to attend your patients day and night. You will have to share their sufferings and their fears, and also face the despair of their loved ones when your efforts have been of no avail. I have followed my profession for so many years and I am getting old and feel very tired, at times, but I have no regrets and I am very happy I have helped so many human beings. This, I feel my duty to tell you. Do not be discouraged if you really feel you want this life, but remember it is a hard one."

He stopped talking and looked at me intently. There was a hint of sadness in his eyes as he said, "I think we should discuss this when you are a bit older, my boy. It is too early yet to make a decision about your future."

Maybe my cherished guardian felt that his health was failing too fast and that I would not have time for long studies. He knew that when he died I would have to be ready to carry the weight of the family, as he had done all his life. A light of kindness and wisdom, which shone on those who knew and loved him, went out with his death. He was a father to his patients and never denied his help to anybody. The poor were his chattels, money had no importance for him. He never accepted payment from those who could not afford it and made them put their money back into their purse, scolding them with kind words. His death was hastened by his spirit of sacrifice. As he lay in bed, suffering with acute bronchitis, a poor desperate man called at our door in the middle of the night. His wife had been in childbirth for endless hours but could not be delivered and the inexperienced young doctor who was attending her was at his wits' end. My guardian left his bed to go out by carriage to the uphill suburb where these poor people lived, to help the unfortunate woman bring her child into the world. The fateful ride into the cold of the night and its consequences on my guardian's already critical condition was one of the reasons that precipitated his death.

I finished high school when I was barely eighteen. I knew my guardian's fondest wish was that I should have gone on with my studies and enter university in England, but he felt his health could not be trusted much longer and did not oppose my decision to look for work. I found employment in an English bank in the city and was very happy not to weigh any more on the family budget. As a matter of fact, I could even help with the household expenses.

Going into employment I found myself in a quite different world. Until then I had lived surrounded by my school friends, my sport partners and companions of fun, but now the atmosphere in which I found myself was very different. The salaried employees around me were people of modest means who had not enjoyed the protected life that had been my share. They had had to fend for themselves all the way and as a consequence had acquired a sterner and more realistic outlook on life. Getting to know my fellow employees was a very positive experience and helped me to develop my individuality, which had perhaps been held in check by the traditional family atmosphere in which I had grown up.

I was assigned to the Loans Department when I started work in the bank. The head of the section was quite a strange kind of person. About fifty and greying at the temples, he was a handsome man of swarthy complexion, a native of Greek origin. Dressed in double-breasted, elegant suits of sober cut, his spare, muscular figure seemed to be made of steel. His eyes, which had a cold icy stare, appeared to be made of the same metal. Usually haughty and stand-offish with everyone, he condescended at times to volunteer the information that in his heyday he had served in the French Foreign Legion. It seemed that, in his opinion, this gave him the right to treat everyone as underlings. I don't think he liked me very much and he lost no opportunity to make me look a fool because of my scant experience of banking and work in general. I suspect that my knowledge of English vexed him considerably, as he could hardly make himself understood in that language. He usually expressed himself in French, which he spoke quite well.

Mr Theodore, since this was the name of this super male, had a very attentive and discerning eye for young ladies and especially for those who, in his opinion, might like a bit of fun. A young Greek telephone operator had been enrolled recently among the female staff. The perfect proportions of this young lady, which her manner of dressing made no effort to conceal, and in particular her magnificent breasts, which she carried erect in constant display, played havoc with the male personnel. Her rosebud mouth, half open to reveal dazzling white teeth, seemed always ready to dispense passionate kisses. Miss Louisa, as this symbol of carnal femininity was called, cast around her such an overpowering and tangible aura of sexuality that when I sometimes came across her in the cloakroom, by mere chance, of course, her perfume as she brushed against me made my legs tremble.

Mr Theodore became immediately aware of this magnificent opportunity and lost no time in starting the hunt. Taking advantage of his position of authority he took every opportunity to enter the frosted glass cage of the telephone switchboard where the young goddess attended to her task. He would come out after a while, rather flushed, with quivering nostrils. It was all too evident: the man of steel had taken a header. One beautiful Sunday morning, as the bank's football team was playing against a minor club eleven, an athletic cyclist appeared on the edge of the pitch. Mr Theodore, for it was him in person, was performing elegant evolutions on a gem of a racing bicycle adorned with a wealth of clever gadgets. He was dressed in white Zouave pantaloons, an off-white, closely fitted singlet which showed his chest muscles to great advantage and a Foreign Legion kepi with a fluttering neck-piece. He reminded us of Beau Geste or Gary Cooper on a bicycle. We, young males, were watching him in amazement and I must confess with a bit of envy. The bicycle was a masterpiece and the costume, if a bit far-fetched, had a lot of swing about it. The luscious telephone operator was looking at him with ill-concealed admiration. In her eyes, we insignificant bank clerks had sunk to the stature of pygmies, buzzing around her. Mr Theodore's manful demonstration had no doubt made a deep breach into Miss Luisa's heart.

After that fateful day, the mature warrior's visits to the glass cage became more assiduous and very soon Mr Theodore's face assumed a greyish hue. His eyes sunk more deeply into their sockets, every day. Then one morning Mr Theodore did not appear at the office and at about midday, a very blond lady, rather extravagantly dressed, materialised in front of my desk. She was tall and rather full in the figure. Her French of good vintage had no Levantine inflexions. It was Mrs Theodore. She was French. She wanted to see the general manager. While waiting to be ushered in, she informed me in an uninterrupted flow of words that she had been born in Morocco where her father held a high governmental position, that she had met Mr Theodore when he was serving in the Legion and had fallen madly in love with him. They were married against her parents' will. She had come to inform the manager that Theodore had fallen off his horse and had a broken leg and an eye almost falling out of its socket. I went to see Mr Theodore that evening.

He lived in a beautiful house in one of the most exclusive residential areas of the town. There was a large garden in front of the elegant entrance. There was also a row of tall plane trees on both sides of the alley that led to the house. The magnificent Arab horse, which he had recently acquired, had wilfully bumped him against one of these plane trees. Most probably this son of the desert was allergic to plane trees. The result of that unfortunate accident was that Mr Theodore had to be absent from work for a long time. As a matter of fact, he never came back. A series of unsavoury facts came to the fore. Mr Theodore accepted graft from bank customers. He granted loans against non-existing commodities.

I do not know how his French wife came to know about his love affair with Miss Luisa and there was a rumour that she threatened to disfigure the young girl with sulphuric acid. Miss Luisa's face went very pale when she heard of this and, from then on, a subtle smell of cold sweat started to mar her captivating body perfume. I had to act as a substitute for Mr Theodore at the bank. The responsibility was too heavy. I had a breakdown after a few weeks and I had to stay at home for some time.

As time passed, the independence I had acquired gave me a great sense of freedom. I soon fell in love with a sweet young secretary who worked at the bank. At eighteen, I believed I had found the love of my life, eternal felicity. Going to work in the morning I was planning matrimony. It was a good half-hour's walk, but the way never seemed too long. I had my head in the clouds. At times however, anxiety invaded my thoughts. What would I have done to keep my wife and children if I ever lost my job? Ours was a very Platonic affair. We certainly wished we could be closer together but it was almost impossible at that time for well-bred young people to be alone together. My sweetheart did not belong to my usual crowd and I could not very well introduce her to my friends. She was a girl of modest upbringing and would have felt out of place. We could not have gone walking together in the country. It was a dangerous thing to do. Native people of Muslim faith imposed great strictures on women's freedom of behaviour. A girl who wandered around, alone with a man in the open country, was in their opinion a woman of no virtue and as such was open to anybody's improper proposals or aggression. Apartment houses were guarded by gruff janitors, ignorant country people with a primitive mentality who looked with suspicion upon any woman who did not inhabit the house. Hotels were out of question. There were very strict rules imposed by the police. Some houses of low repute existed, of course, in the suburbs but they were situated in such ill-famed neighbourhoods as to discourage any desire to venture into them. Besides, how could we pure-minded youngsters muster enough cold-blooded courage to think of dragging our beloved into a situation that left no doubt as to the end that was contemplated. Things could and did happen sometimes under favourable circumstances, but it was always preferable to enjoy the benefit of spontaneity. There was nothing very much one could do at the cinema. Everybody's eyes were fixed on one's back and besides it was not done to go to the cinema in pairs. A girl lost her reputation. At most young lovers could look at each other with tenderness, hold hands and steel a kiss behind some secluded corner.

Every morning, before going to work, I bought a red rose for my beloved. I hid the flower in my hat. One day, this idyll came to an end. The girl told me it could not go on like this. I was too young to marry her and she firmly believed in marriage. Later I fell in love again and every time I thought it was the real thing. How wonderful to love when one is young, though one often suffers unquenched desire or jealousy because of a smile bestowed upon some other. The sadness comes when the heart is empty, deprived of love and love's torment.

I used to play tennis at an English Club, which had a number of good, red earth, hard courts and a club house, in a disused military barracks training ground, right in the middle of the residential quarter of the European district. Tennis in those days was somewhat of a snobbish sport with strict rules of dressing and behaviour. Whites had to be worn on the courts without exceptions. A white shirt and flannel trousers, cotton trousers were hardly tolerated. The club's promoters, mostly British residents born in Turkey, had kept very closely to their tradition and transformed it in to a small piece of England. There was tea at five o'clock and conversation was held at as low a pitch as possible.

In 1924, taking advantage of the presence of many foreigners in town, the club organised an International Tennis Tournament. There were many good tennis players among the diplomats of the various foreign embassies, consulates and legations at Constantinople, as well as among the managing staff of the various international enterprises that had opened branches in Turkey, and the event could be rightly defined as international. What I well remember, since it struck me particularly as I watched the players, was the very dissimilar styles of tennis displayed by the various competitors. Tennis in those days had not yet assumed the uniform aspect that is now so common. Players distinguished themselves not only by their own personal way of performing a shot, but also by keeping to the characteristic style of game practised by their nation. Usual shots, like the service, drives and volleys, were played in a very different manner by competitors.

A spry, middle-aged American gentleman served in a most unorthodox manner. He threw the ball well in front of him and brought it back with a spoon-like lunge of his racket, hitting it flat with a reverse cut. On landing on the opposite side of the net, the ball shied away backwards from his opponent. Russians and Romanians lifted their forehand drives very considerably, hitting the ball hard with their rackets held flat, facing the other side. Japanese and Czechoslovaks cut their balls to a slither and caused them to die breathless on the court. The French played a brilliant game, volleying and smashing their heart's content.

Volleys were generally placed very cunningly and played softly. Back-hand drives were generally cut by most players. Service was performed by most Mittel-European players with more force than swing and standing squarely facing the net. The British, Germans and Austrians played a more classic, almost modern style of tennis, but if I may say so, it was more interesting to watch. It was always full of individuality and intelligence. The Turkish and native-born competitors managed quite well. Their style of game differed according to the opportunity they had had of observing foreign players.

It was a beautiful sight to watch the agile performers moving swiftly on the well-kept courts. There was also a great show of elegance and gentility. British players contributed greatly to this by arriving on the courts wearing magnificent blazers with light or dark blue stripes, according to the university at which they had studied. Tall and athletic, they sported long-peaked cricket caps assorted to their blazers and invariably carried half a dozen rackets under their arms, as tennis champions still do today.

There was a great delusion at the end of the tournament. Almost a scandal. The men's singles were won by a modest, unobtrusive Armenian tennis player who owned a small restaurant in the vicinity. He sometimes wore a non-too freshly laundered white shirt and had only one racket.

Time was passing. I had just turned twenty when my guardian's health started to give him serious trouble. He was no doubt very much aware of his severe condition and decided there and then to travel to Vienna and go into a clinic. His wife's two brothers, my maternal uncles, lived there and managed a small bank. My guardian's modest savings had been entrusted to them and I suppose my guardian's idea was also to be able to make the necessary arrangements about his legacy.

I fully realised that his life was near its end. The thought of losing him caused me great anguish. The deep feeling which bound me to this exceptional being, who cared for me like a loving father and had always been my spiritual guide, was so predominant in my affections as to supersede the natural sentiment of kinship I had for my mother and sister. The news reaching us about my guardian's health got steadily worse, until he finally wrote to tell us to sell everything that was of any value in the house and join him in Vienna. We would have lived there with my mother's brother who had a large, richly furnished flat, where nothing we could have brought with us would be really wanted.

It was sad to part with all the things that represented the home we had lived in. There were many objects that were dearer to us than others, but conditions made it necessary to try and increase the family's modest resources as much as possible with the proceeds of the sale. However, we did not sell the beautiful Georgian bronze mantle clock, which used to soothe my midnight fears with its friendly ticking. It is a prized heirloom and it still stands in front of me, in my study. My guardian had inherited it from his grandfather who was a purveyor to the Sultan's estates.

Our departure from Constantinople was a sharp break with the past. We were leaving the place where we were born, where we had grown up. We were parting from our friends and relatives and from the places we loved. The environment in which we had lived was of a very particular nature. Although we were born and had always lived in Turkey, we belonged to a separate group of people that, although settled in Turkey for five centuries, had not absorbed the physiognomy of the nation that gave it hospitality. The Sephardi Jewish community, although completely free in its adopted country, lived in a kind of voluntary invisible enclosure. Constantly and closely in contact with the population at large, it formed a separate ethnic entity which kept to strict rules of custom and behaviour.

A Sephardi Jew had many friends outside his community, and difference in faith and nationality was of no importance in everyday life, but he would never marry out of his religious group and there was a sort of invisible barrier that materialised on some issues at times. The Sephardi Spanish Jews formed a separate caste and had preserved, almost unaltered, the ways and peculiarities of their original Spanish homeland, from which they had been exiled because they would not abjure the religion of their fathers.

In common with the other ethnic minorities, namely the Greeks and Armenians who lived in Turkey, the Jews kept apart from the Muslim population. This state of things was in no manner enforced by the local authorities. It was a status quo that came in very handy to both sides. The Greeks, Armenians and Jews could keep their language, religion and customs and the Muslims were in no danger of being contaminated by these infidels. Provided that no freedom-seeking, anti-Turkish ideologies were voiced or practised, the authorities representing the Sultan tried not to obscure the image of tolerance, which had been the prerogative of the more illuminated forms of Islam. Efforts were made to maintain an attitude of benevolence and fairness towards the non-Muslim minorities, and this included giving them the possibility of putting their talents at the disposal of the government in the administration of the country. There were non-Muslims in exalted positions as advisers, lawyers, financial experts, doctors and engineers. There was also a willingness to show consideration to these minorities, giving them an opportunity to appear at official ceremonies in honour of the Sultan.

On Fridays, the Muslim day of prayer, it was customary to invite the representatives of the various faiths to the military ceremony that took place in front of the Mosque where the Sultan attended to his religious duties. In good time, in the morning, four state coaches left the palace with an escort of four lancers, in full uniform, on their way to collect the Greek Orthodox Metropolitan, the Armenian Bishop, the Chief Rabbi and the Monsignor, the Apostolic Nuncio, who took care of the religious health of foreigners professing the Catholic faith. These high dignitaries were taken to attend the Sultan's parade in front of the mosque where the Sultan was praying surrounded by his ministers and court officials. Meanwhile, the Sultan's bodyguard, in their coloured, gold-braided uniforms, would sit rigidly, like toy soldiers, on their beautifully groomed horses. On such occasions the Diplomatic Corps in its entirety would be invited to the ceremony and the gala uniforms, the plumed cocked hats and shiny top hats would add splendour to the pageant. Some of the Byzantine customs and systems of government had remained latent in the Ottoman Empire's administration after the conquest of Constantinople by Mahomet II in 1453. The model set by the Byzantine Basileus of favouring the orderly living together of the various ethnic minorities, and allowing them a certain measure of self-government, was followed by the new Ottoman rulers and had given good results.

The Sephardi Jewish communities had kept faithfully to the use of the Spanish language, which was also largely practised in the city's world of commerce by other ethnic minorities in their dealings with those Jews who spoke only Ladino and expressed themselves badly in Turkish. These people, cast out from Spain where they had lived for almost a thousand years and then welcomed and tolerated in Turkey during the reign of Bayezid II at the end of the fifteenth century, continued to live in accordance with the customs they had brought with them. In certain attitudes, they had also conserved a grain of haughty pride of pure Spanish stamp. They had enjoyed the privilege of never having to bow their head to anyone, having preferred exile to slavery. The condition of absolute religious freedom they enjoyed in Turkey had resulted in a completely different attitude to that of the majority of the Diaspora, where repression and persecution had favoured the development of blind orthodoxy. Though adamantly keeping faith to the Commandments of the Law, they practised their Judaism with less tenacious obstinacy, because they could profess their belief openly.

Before leaving for Vienna I went to take my leave from my Uncle Joseph, my father's brother, an observant and religious man, who had taken upon himself to supervise my allegiance to religious duties. On Yom Kippur day I used to go to his house and accompany him to the synagogue. When the blessing was imparted by the officiant, I squeezed myself under his prayer shawl with my two cousins. Under the influence of his religiousness I felt more deeply the significance and solemnity of the Day of Atonement. I realised more fully the importance of assuming responsibility for one's own errors and, by asking personally for the forgiveness of those offended, of feeling purified and at peace with oneself, Staying with my Uncle Joseph, I felt the awakening of a religious sentiment that gave me comfort and strength.

We were not very observant of the ritual dietary rules in our home. My guardian was averse to a custom which in his opinion had lost its meaning in present times. He had studied medicine at the Faculty in Leipzig at a time of great iconoclastic upheaval and had returned home with very revolutionary ideas about ritual religiousness. He was against set rules and anachronistic restrictions, which he deemed were an obstacle to the freedom of thought. In his absolute faith in self-determination and man's indisputable right to act in accordance with his own conscience, he could not admit the necessity of rites and ceremonies and the unquestioned obedience to any code of religion. He willingly discussed the Torah and Talmud, which he often consulted and interpreted in his own way, with men of religious knowledge and with some rabbis who were open to dialogue, but he would invariably scandalise them with his unorthodox and somewhat reckless theories. He did not feel, however, that he had the right to condition my Jewish conscience by his way of thinking and dutifully sent me to my Uncle Joseph's house to have a bath of religious observance.

However, my guardian's human behaviour, in the moral sense of the word, could have served as an example to many strict observants of the rites of their faith. He was fully aware of the spiritual magnitude of Judaism and conscious of the social and the human significance of the teachings of the Law and the Decalogue, of the observance of charity and the revolutionary purport of the Sabbatical Laws and the Jubilee, which set the canons of humanity and social justice among men. He spoke proudly of these Laws and explained their social meaning to those who, although observant of the ritual form of our faith, had never yet fathomed the depth of its wisdom. He had a boundless sense of humanity and worked ceaseless for relief and charitable institutions. I don't think anybody had ever knocked at his door to ask for advice, medical assistance or money without having found help and understanding. My guardian's lack of ritual observance and his informal religious conception did not in anyway cause me to lose anything of the moral significance of Judaism.

In the narrow observance of the ritual discipline of every religion there is maybe, for those who feel its necessity, a mystical component that carries them beyond the mechanism of prayer. The compelling urge felt by Jews to conform strictly to their ritual discipline is undoubtedly brought about by the example set by their father, by their love for his person or their respect for his memory. There is also often a desire to express their own religious sentiments in a tangible manner.

In the less orthodox climate of the Sephardic home, where daily conversation in traditional Ladino is abundantly interspersed with proverbs and sayings from the Torah, and where the spiritual meaning of festivities and religious commandments is openly discussed by grown-ups and their elders in the presence of women and children, my sense of Jewishness developed itself forcefully, though I never felt the desire to express it ritually. I think I have absorbed more Jewish teaching in this way, than the little I was able to learn from the young rabbi who taught me the prayers in Hebrew I had to recite on the occasion of my Bar-Mitzvah, the religious coming of age of every Jewish boy at the age of thirteen.

At later times I have always tried to deepen my knowledge of the Law and its significant moral teaching, thinking instinctively in my intimate conscience that I would have to transmit it to my children. I feel however, that I did not discover much more than what my mind and my feelings had already and instinctively imbued through an atavism I felt very strongly. All the same, in the process of learning more about the teachings of the Elders, I felt with joy and more awareness the importance of the legacy in which I had a share and which encouraged me to give, above all, free course to my sentiment of humanity which was part of my nature as a result of the example I was set and because of my conscious attitude.

In the very varied company of my teenage friends, many of whom were of different faiths, I was able to learn what was right and worthwhile in their particular religion. A Jew in Turkey never felt that he was constrained in a ghetto. On the same plane as an Orthodox Christian or a Catholic he could practise his religion in full liberty. As for the Muslim lords of the country, although professing that the only true doctrine was faith in Allah, the religiousness of these hosts was a praiseworthy quality which Jews respected.

Uncle Joseph had a warehouse in which he sold woollen cloth that he imported from England. It was situated in one of those huge labyrinthine buildings, in the higher part of Istanbul's commercial area, where this kind of trade was carried on. He was known as an honest and dependable merchant who was an expert in his trade. When I went to take leave from him before departing for Vienna to join my guardian, I found him, sitting at his desk, in the cubicle at the very end of his warehouse. He looked sadly at me. He was distressed and had a presentiment of his brother's death.

"Come up with me," he said after a while, "I want to give you some cloth for a heavy cloak. The winter is cold in Vienna."

We went up the narrow stairs to the first floor. There were heavy rolls of woollen cloth on a very massive bench. I stopped in front of a bolt of grey cloth with an unobtrusive pattern.

Uncle Joseph looked at me and his eyes were full of tears. "It is better you should choose some black cloth," he said.

As I kissed him to say goodbye, I too was in tears. I felt his hand upon my head as he was saying the blessing in Hebrew. I had never felt a blessing hand on my head before and was deeply moved.

My guardian died on the day after our arrival in Vienna. It was as if he had been waiting for us. He remained fully conscious up to the end. We were all around him when he breathed for the last time. I had never seen a human being die before and when he fell back lifeless on his bed, I had the vivid impression I had seen his soul depart from the body. It was as if the spark of life, which God had put in him, had been suddenly extinguished, leaving behind a limp corpse of no significance. As we took him to the cemetery I did not feel I had lost him. We had not parted. His spirit was with me. I wore his clothes for a long time. They gave me comfort.

In Vienna we lived in my Uncle Albert's flat. He was my mother's brother. Uncle Albert looked very much like a good giant. His large size was in great contrast with his gentle ways. He managed a small bank in the Rotenturmstrasse which belonged to him and his brother Victor. He had integrated himself so completely in his position as chairman that he wore a morning coat and did his best to hide his true easy-going nature under an earnest and somewhat solemn, appearance. We used to go to work together every morning. We often joked when we were alone and shared a laugh together about the same subject: for example, the undisputed dominion of the women in our house.

There were five of them. Three aunts, my mother and my sister. Two aunts were widows and with my mother they made three. Another of the aunts was a spinster and had long lost her bloom but not the hope of finding a husband. I thought my poor sister was in great danger of losing her freshness in that company.

We, men, were heavily outnumbered and could not possibly voice an opinion, without being immediately contrasted by one or the other of the ladies of the house. Our only salvation was in our escape to work every morning. We always tried to find an excuse not to return home for lunch. There was a self-service a few yards away from the bank. It was a great novelty a revolutionary thing in those days in Vienna. It was called Express, and it offered a godsend of varied canapés, with or without mayonnaise, hot würstel and jellied chicken. All these delicacies were on view behind glass, in small compartments that opened automatically when a coin was placed in a slot by the side of the small glass door. Cold beer, wine, boiling tea or coffee would be dispensed on demand, too, out of brightly polished copper taps, surmounted by their metal labels, with the assistance, naturally of the requested coin.

Uncle Albert had a very cultivated mind and I enjoyed talking to him. He had a perfect knowledge of French and German and knew Arabic and Persian as well. He had been a high school teacher of Oriental languages in his youth in Constantinople where he was born. For his own enjoyment and at the slightest provocation, and perhaps also for my own pleasure, he would start reciting long excerpts from the best poetical works of Lamartine, or Victor Hugo, or Goethe and Schiller beautifully and without the faintest lapse of memory. Sometimes he would even recite works in Persian. I did not understand the language but I liked the sound of it. He did not do this out of lack of modesty. He enjoyed hearing his own voice. He would have made a good actor, maybe, had he not been born in a bourgeois family, which considered the theatre a den of perdition.

I did very little work at the bank in Vienna. I had an office all to myself on the first floor, where the receiving rooms were situated. They were generally empty. Leaving the door of my office slightly ajar

I could peep into the telephone operator's cabin. She was a jolly girl, well shaped and of friendly disposition. When she realised I had an eye for her we became fast friends very soon. She was typically Viennese, full of life, and loved to have a good time. She taught me a lot of things.

I stayed in Vienna for some months. I had qualms of conscience for not trying to improve the material welfare of my family now that I was responsible for it. The decision was finally taken that I should join my Uncle Victor in Milan who had often insisted I should come and help him in the Oriental carpet business he had established there. Italy was quite a foreign part of the world to me. I did not know its language and had never found an opportunity to learn anything about its history after the decline of the Roman Empire. I knew of the existence of Milan. In the preface of *Le Rouge et le Noir* I had read that Stendhal had been French Consul in that city and liked it very much.

I left Vienna with my Uncle Albert. We boarded a sleeper that left the city in the evening and would arrive in Milan the next day. Waking up on the train in the morning we realised we were already in Italy. The landscape was quite different. The deep woods and green meadows of Ketten had been left behind. A rolling plain extended itself down to the horizon where, through the morning mist, a chain of snow-topped mountains could just be seen, emerging from banks of thick white clouds. As we neared a station the train came slowly to a halt.

"Have a look outside and see where we are," said Uncle Albert.

Looking through the window still frosted by the cold of the night, I could distinguish a large poster. "We are at Uscita,"[12] I told Uncle Albert.

He seemed quite puzzled by the name of this city.

We arrived in Milan early in the afternoon. It was a beautiful day at the end of May. The station stood on a sort of a low embankment and I seem to remember there was a tree-bordered alley leading to it. We stayed at the Hotel Diana in Viale Piave. There was a garden at the back of the hall where we had dinner. There was also an orchestra and the guests danced in the evening on a small platform among the tables. The multicoloured lights illuminating the garden were dipped when the orchestra played a tango.

The extensive warehouse in which my Uncle Victor conducted his Oriental carpets business was situated on the first and only floor of a largish old house, which stood at the corner of what at that time was called Piazzetta Durini. Today an imposing compound of tall buildings towers up on this spot, housing a gallery lined with elegant shops. A well-known bar and pastry shop, the Gin Rosa occupies one of its corners. When I arrived in Milan in 1927, the ground floor of that old house, which had its front on four intersecting thoroughfares – Corso Venezia, Corso Vittorio Emanuele, Via Durini and

---

[12] *Uscita*: way out.

Via Montenapoleone – was leased to a large café called Moka Efti, decorated in make-believe Oriental style, where an outlandish character wearing a red fez served Turkish coffee at small, three-legged, round tables with incised yellow brass tops. The tables stood on the pavement. For the less exotically minded customers it was also possible to enjoy a good espresso or a frothy cappuccino and crispy brioches.

The entrance to the warehouse was at the back of the café, in the piazzetta, and a rather narrow staircase led up to a small landing, almost completely filled by a door with a frosted glass upper pane on which, painted in brilliant yellow, a rampant lion wielded a curved sabre against a background of a flaming setting sun. Over the lion's head were the words, "Oriental Carpets – Direct Importers". Beside the doorknob, a small, elongated, white enamel plate bore the words "Come in" in black letters. As the door was pushed open, a bell dangling over it trilled with a lingering sound.

Uncle Victor's unmistakable voice reached our ears as we entered the place. He was holding forth, standing on top of a disorderly mass of rugs of all descriptions. Quick as lightning, he was pulling out some more rugs from the orderly piles covering the floor of the large room and throwing them with a flourish in front of his bemused customers, before having them spread out in proper order by his assistants.

Oriental carpets were hardly known to the general public in Italy at that time and it took a hammering technique of relentless persuasion to overcome their reticence. Uncle Victor was a prodigy of salesmanship. His inexhaustible loquacity, interspersed with salacious wit, mesmerised his audience. As he saw us, he stopped talking for a moment, hugged us affectionately and resumed his monologue for the benefit of his clients.

The warehouse looked like a battlefield. Three porters were continuously readjusting the orderly carpet piles that had been ransacked by my uncle. As I started to help uncle Victor in his work, I could not restrain his all-embracing, overflowing activity. He wanted to do everything himself. As time went on, he learned to trust me. He was quite satisfied in the end to have somebody he could lean on and who could give him a hand. He had never had a son and it seemed as if, in a certain way, I was filling this void for him. At night, in summer, when I was already in bed, he would come to fetch me for a long walk through the city. He made me part of his business projects. His mind was aglow with new ideas which were quite often not commercially sound enough to be carried out and I had all the trouble in the world to talk him out of his most ill-judged enterprises.

It was in Milan that I finally attained complete independence. My mother and sister had remained in Vienna and although I usually spent my days with my uncle and had my meals at his house, I slept for the first time in my own quarters. Life in Milan was very much to my liking. We had two motorcars, which were necessary for our business, and I was learning to drive.

There were many lovely girls around and having a car was a real asset. I soon found out, however, that things were not as easy as they seemed. Girls in Milan had little in common with those in Vienna. They all wanted a marriage proposal before starting any kind of substantial flirt and as a young and inexperienced foreigner I was not up for that game. I could not possibly swear everlasting marital love to the first young person who drew my fancy. Uncle Victor looked on, with great amusement, at my fruitless efforts to find myself a girl. Such matters did not represent the least problem for him. He had various affairs going on at the same time and he kept me wondering at the skill with which he got out of the most embarrassing predicaments. He was capable of keeping perfectly cool in the most intricate situations. He had the courage of a lion and a gift for solving the various muddles he got himself into, without batting an eyelid.

It was the time of the first years of Hitler's accession to power, when Jews in Germany still had the choice of leaving their homeland on condition that they renounced most of their fortune. Vast numbers of Jews came to Italy at this time, either wishing to stay in the country permanently or to emigrate to the United States.

One fine day, an elderly, very distinguished couple came to see my uncle at his office. They had a letter of introduction from a good friend of his in Vienna. With them was their daughter. She was lovely, in her late twenties and full of seductive charm. Uncle Victor immediately fell prey to her wiles. As a matter of fact, he had never in his life resisted the lure of a beautiful woman. These good people told my uncle that they had left a considerable sum, the better part of what they possessed, in cash, with some trusted friends in Berlin, as they were afraid of smuggling it out of Germany. If the money had been found on them they would have been sent to a concentration camp. Their friends in Germany were ready to hand the money over to a person who gave them the agreed password. They came to ask my uncle if it would be possible to find an honest smuggler, who in exchange for a very substantial fee, would run the risk of bringing the money to Italy and then deliver it to them, instead of keeping it for himself after crossing the frontier. Uncle Victor did not know if such a person even existed, and he told them so.

He got into the habit of visiting the old couple and their lovely daughter quite often and used to disappear from work to go and see them at a small hotel where they had settled, not far from Via Montenapoleone. A short time went by and then he said to me one morning: "You know, Victor, I think I should take a trip to Berlin. There are certainly lots of beautiful carpets to be bought there now that so many merchants have to dispose of their stocks in a hurry."

I was not very taken with his intention to travel to Berlin, but it would have been no use to try and talk him out of the project. There was no way of getting him to desist from any enterprise in which he saw an element of personal risk. He enjoyed courting danger. Uncle Victor left for Berlin that same night. I had no inkling, at that moment, of his new friends' money problem and if I had, knowing my uncle's nature, I would have certainly been more concerned about his trip to Germany. Three days went by and he reappeared. His face showed signs of great stress and tiredness but he was in exceptionally high spirits. He had not bought any carpets but he could not hide the fact that he was very pleased with himself.

"Come," he said to me. "Let's go and have a cup of coffee."

As soon as we were seated, his eyes shining with excitement, he started to tell me, not sparing any detail, how he had tricked the hated Nazis and brought back his friends' money hoard, saving them from a life of poverty. Now they would be able to emigrate to America and build themselves a new future. The money had been handed over to him by their faithful friends in Berlin without any trouble. The large sum was in banknotes of the highest denomination. Before leaving Milan he had taken care to procure the necessary equipment. He had taken with him three large, canvas-backed envelopes and strong sheets of cardboard cut to size. In addition, he had a bottle of China ink, a small brush and a tube of fast-acting adhesive paste given to him by a dentist friend. He had also not forgotten to take along a pair of black cotton gloves.

Towards evening the next day, after ascertaining that he had not been followed, he made his way to the station. The train for Italy left at half-past eight in the evening. He arrived much earlier at the station and as the train reached the platform he rushed into a third-class carriage. As he had foreseen, its compartment were empty. The three envelopes containing the banknotes had been duly blackened with the ink and were now sprinkled with adhesive and stuck under the wooden seat of one of the compartments, far back, close to the partition. Having finished his work, he got rid of his gloves and the tube of adhesive paste, throwing them in two different litter bins, bought a bottle of beer and a couple of sandwiches and then ensconced himself in the corner seat of a second-class carriage not far from where he had placed the money and pretended he had gone to sleep. It was obvious that the S.S. would have flashed their torches under the seats to check for travellers' suitcases and packages, but it was improbable they would have concentrated the beam on the underside of the seat so far at the back. Besides, the envelopes were black and did not stick out that much above the surface.

Arriving at Milan, not without a few moments of anxiety, he had waited for the carriage to empty and then recovered the envelopes with immense relief.

The strain had hold even on Uncle Victor's nerves of steel, but the elation he felt at having accomplished the dangerous feat pushed everything into the background. The old couple was overjoyed to be out of their troubles and did not know how to repay my uncle who would not even accept repayment for the price of his ticket to Berlin.

It is not out of malice, but I still believe that Uncle Victor's good deed, although motivated in the first place by his kind heart and his desire for adventure, had a lot to do with his keen interest in the lovable, young daughter of his newly acquired friends. The sentiment was reciprocated, and I well remember the looks that the enchantress lavished on my uncle. Who knows how many times she asked him to tell her the story of his mad adventure, in private of course.

Not long after my arrival in Milan, my uncle decided I had to transfer myself to Florence to keep an eye on a small branch office we had opened there in Via Cavour, entrusted to one of our employees. Things did not seem to run as they should and the purpose of my journey was to decide whether we should keep this office open or not. I confess that after a few days in Florence I lost all desire to think about business matters. I fell under the spell of that enchanting city and tried to find all sorts of reasons to prolong my stay in Florence. I used to go for long walks in the Tuscan countryside and motored to its remotest corners. It seemed to me I was travelling in a world that had not changed for centuries.

Siena was bathed in the sun's splendour as I arrived there at noon. The Piazza del Palio was deserted. No sound lingered in the air and the windows of the surrounding *palazzi* looked on with spent eyes. Out of a low porch, all of a sudden sauntered a little man. He was dressed like a medieval jester. I stood dumbfounded, carried back into time. As he had appeared, the little man vanished after a few moments, swallowed like a ghost into the depths of a sombre, tortuous alley.

I stopped for lunch at a small trattoria not far away from the Piazza. As I told the host about my strange encounter, he burst out laughing. The little man, he explained, was a famous *cantastorie*, an itinerant kind of bard, who wore the costume in order to better illustrate the medieval legends he recounted, helping the imagination of his audience with naive posters he carried in his baggage, which conjured up the castles, the beautiful dames and the brave knights who were the subjects of his tales.

Driving on through the enchanting countryside, I stopped to visit Assisi. I was resting for a while, away from the summer heat, sitting on a low wall under a shady tree, when a graceful young woman came to sit not far away from me. It was not long before we got talking. She came from Scotland and was very pleased to have found somebody who spoke her own language. In those days, the beautiful sights of this world had not yet been infested by chattering tourists speaking every possible tongue. She lived in Florence, studied painting and was on her own. It did not seem possible that I had finally met a girl to my liking, a twin soul to share the joys of being young in a world where the magic of the surrounding countryside was almost a physical sensation, charged with unspoilt beauty and alive with history. We decided, there and then, to continue our wanderings together.

I have still in my eyes the soft image of the mellow coloured landscape, the ruined castles on top of the hills, surmounting quaint villages, built around them like beehives. The tall cypresses turning blue as the sun set. At night we passed through sleeping hamlets. The roar of the motor-car engine sounded like sacrilege in that dormant world. The wonderful adventure left a deep mark, an unforgettable memory in my young soul, which was yet unpolluted by the less poetical adventures of my later bachelor life.

A year went by and my mother and sister came to join me in Milan. We were now definitely settled in Italy. I liked living in Milan. The people were warm-hearted and open to foreigners. I also took an increasing interest in my work and tried to bring more knowledge and professionalism to this particular trade. Such purposeful trends were not common in those days. We were now dealing mostly with private customers and I was getting to know a group of well-established customers, who were soundly educated and well mannered, from the higher bourgeoisie of Milan, the backbone of the country.

I used to travel very often, mostly to the northern part of Italy. There was very little traffic on the roads at the time. Leaving Milan from Piazzale Loreto, where the urban centre almost ended, one proceeded through tree-lined Viale Padova and then found oneself already on the highway north. At night there was the hazard of the heavy horse carts, which more than often travelled in the middle of the road. Straining one's ears one caught, barely in time, the faint metallic sound of iron-rimmed wheels and dangling chains. The dim light of a lantern see-sawed under the cart, where the drunk driver sprawled fast asleep on the heap of sand he transported. The tired horse plodded on, unheeded. He knew his way to the stable.

As I fell asleep after returning from my long forays in the country, an endless procession of dusty roads, plane tree avenues, ubiquitous church spires, villages and towns passed through the turmoil of my tired mind before I could close my eyes.

For my first holiday in Italy, I went to Abbazia on the Adriatic Coast. The year was 1927 and this enchanted spot was still the favourite sea resort, the paradise of the Mittel-European affluent class. The various languages of the late Austro-Hungarian Empire were heard all over the place: German with Austrian softness, Hungarian, melodious on women's lips, Slavic languages of various inflections, Polish and Czech. The foreign women were free and unconstrained, often full of enterprise. Italian girls, in contrast, even in this permissive atmosphere kept

111

the reserved, sometimes prim attitude to which they had to conform at home. The sea was beautiful and inviting and I revelled in it, going for long swims. I felt a wonderful sense of freedom in the water. At times I motored to Fiume, a few miles away. From the Italian border separating this town from the Yugoslav frontier at Susak, I could watch the Slavic frontier guards. They looked to me rough and sullen, in no way like the jolly, carefree, young soldiers who manned the Italian border crossing.

I had a company of pleasant friends in Milan. We went dancing to open-air, popular beer halls or revelled in some small trattoria around a fiasco of good wine, eating salami and mortadella. Our group was not very mixed. There were many young men and too few girls. Only the more experienced and mature in our lot had a steady companion and brought her along. Sometimes an uninhibited model or young seamstress, looking for fun, would join our not-so-wild stag parties. We went back home late at night. We would sing on the way, but stopped to listen when a well-known aria, sung with proficiency by a fresh voiced great tenor of the future, filled the silence with its pure beauty. Thus passed the time of our youth.

The clouds were gathering in the sky, ugly dark clouds, which heralded the storm that swept over our world, taking with our generation's joy of living. The last two years before the declaration of the 1939–45 War was the most distressing period I can remember. Every day I felt a deadly snare was inexorably closing more tightly around our lives. At the door of my shop in Via Montenapoleone, where I had transferred my business a few years earlier, and over which the shop-sign with my name left no doubt as to my origin, German Jewish refugees would appear almost every day. Men and women, young and old, with a tired and hopeless look in their eyes: human derelicts. They had been ousted from their homes and had only saved their lives by precipitous flight. Most of them were without any means at all and they asked for help to survive, to find a meal and a roof. Above all they needed somewhere to stay, a country that would give them refuge, a place where they could continue to live. They knew they were not wanted anywhere and that it would be fatal if they fell into Nazi hands again. We did all we could to provide for their most urgent needs, to intervene in their favour in order to prolong their temporary permit to stay in Italy, but it was almost impossible to help them to emigrate, away from Europe.

These poor people, uprooted, humiliated and deprived of means of subsistence, had lost their faith in themselves and in their future. Their will was destroyed and most of them had fallen into sullen despair. Having been fully assimilated into a country in which they believed they were equal to any other German, most of the younger people had lost that eternal spark of Jewishness, the spark that would have always kept alive in their soul a belief and hope in the providence of the Almighty which never abandons a Jew until he dies. They were ashamed to be Jewish, infected as they were by the disparagement to which they had been submitted. Above all, it was necessary to restore them to a psychic equilibrium in order to enable them to believe that everything was not lost, that there were still human beings who would offer them understanding and kindness and kindle a new hope in their hearts. The more fortunate among them managed to find a haven in the New World, while others entered Palestine after endless vicissitudes. However, most of them wandered from one country to another, in Europe, and finally fell into the hands of the Nazis and were put to death in extermination camps.

The time had come for us to leave Italy. I was conscious that around us, the walls of a prison were rising higher and higher. A prison from which there would be no escape. Anger was rising in my soul. A primeval instinct to fight the evil of German barbarism, to react again the hateful enemy who was denying us our right to live.

It was cold and rainy as we left Milan on that morning in May 1939, on our way to England.

114

Chapter Four

W e were very silent, my mother, my wife Laure and I, on the train which was taking us away from our home, our friends and the country where we had married and lived happily for so many years. We were conscious of facing the unknown, the throes of a war that seemed more inevitable every day and the anguish of separation when I would have to join the army. I was also very worried about our limited financial resources, which would not have kept my mother and my wife for that long through a prolonged period of war, cut off as we were from the major part of our assets, which we had had to leave behind in Italy.

When we arrived in London we were lucky to find accommodation in a small boarding house on Cromwell Road, which had been recommended to us by some friends. The boarding house, like most buildings in that neighbourhood, had two storeys, a ground floor and a basement that was accessible from the street down a short flight of stone stairs that led into a narrow area. The basement had high windows that let in much of the daylight and a frosted glass-panelled door. Tradesmen used that door to deliver their goods and an array of milk bottles could be seen in front of it in the morning. The main door was three steps up from the pavement, under a portico flanked by two columns. The boarding house owner was a Tuscan by origin who had been brought to England as a child. He now added the good-natured, easy ways of his Italian background to his formal English manners.

Our bedrooms, at the back of the house, looked over a small garden, which bordered on a large wooded expanse belonging to an imposing, elegant villa whose front was on the wide road parallel to ours. In the morning we could hear the birds twittering on our window sill and watch the top of the large trees gleaming in the sunlight.

A school friend of mine, Basil Constantinidis, with whom I had kept in touch over the years, lived in London with his wife Eileen. They were our closest link with our new surroundings and we usually spent weekends with them. I went to work every day in my friend's office. He imported tinned goods for local consumption: tomatoes, sardines, vegetables and fruit. I was impressed by the enormous quantities of tinned foods that were needed in England. My particular assignment was to canvass shopkeepers and trade wholesalers on the outskirts of the city and in the neighbouring suburbs. I was completely worn out and mortified on going back home in the evening. I was deeply humiliated at having to deal with rough persons who did not mince their words, after having dealt in my profession with the refined, upper class people who used to visit my shop in Milan and with whom I entertained friendly relations on an equal footing. My friend in London could not offer me anything that would have suited me better. His partner had come up all the way from junior salesman and could not imagine how I could have qualms about waiting long hours to be admitted, only to be dismissed, all too often and none too gently, having achieved nothing. He had gone through that for years. Why shouldn't I? It was not my kind of world and I used to come back to the boarding house very depressed, to join my wife and my mother who were very lonely and felt the ache of having left behind so many things which had given meaning to their life.

The months were going by and the evil of enemy invasion had cast its pall over Central Europe. One after the other, Austria and Czechoslovakia fell under the Nazi heel. On 1 September 1939 Hitler invaded Poland. Then on 3 September, Great Britain declared war on Germany to honour the bond she had signed. Barrage balloons soared up into the air, tethered to the ground by long steel cables. Against the clear London sky, on these beautiful autumn days the oblong silvery shapes looked like festive ornaments.

At about half-past eleven that same morning the air-raid alarm was sounded. People looked at each other quizzically, but if there was any apprehension it did not show on anybody's face. It was a false alarm. The suspected airplane turned out to be one of ours coming back from a mission.

People had not yet become war conscious. There were few soldiers around. In accordance with tradition the army had always been kept to a minimum in peacetime and the Territorial reservists were still mostly in training. Home Guard units were immediately formed. They consisted of men who were mainly over military age. They marched daily in the parks and trained with dummy guns or the few firearms they could lay their hands on, mostly hunting rifles and old army revolvers. I had applied to enlist in the army as soon as I arrived in England but was told my age group was not being called up yet and, as I had no former military experience, I would have to wait for my turn. Twenty-three-year-olds were going into service and I was thirty-three.

The winter of 1939 went by and one day in spring I read in the newspaper that the army was looking for personnel who knew languages. I went to the given address the next day. The unobtrusive building looked a bit mysterious and there was nothing military about its appearance. There was a small sign on the side of the door, which read 'Field Security'. A soldier siting at the entrance sent me to the first floor. I was interviewed by a friendly officer who tested my language proficiency in French, German and Italian.

He seemed satisfied with the result and finally said, "Thank you very much. Please keep yourself at our disposal. You will be notified when you are wanted."

As I was leaving the place, I asked the soldier at the door, "Could you tell me what Field Security means?"

He shook his head and said, "I really don't know."

The summer went by and I had not heard anything from Field Security. Then at the beginning of September the London Blitz began. Air raids followed one another every night and often during the day. The first attack on London started in the afternoon and by that night the docks along the Thames and a large portion of the City were a mass of flames. The next day the streets were covered with broken glass and smoking ruins.

After this London was subjected to a continuous hammering. It started as darkness fell in the evening and continued until dawn. Londoners reacted with great courage in this adversity. They refused to allow the life of the city to be upset. The only difference was that people moving about in the streets carried a square cardboard box, worn over the shoulders. It contained a gas mask. There were more ruins every day and blocked areas, but everyone just pretended it was normal. In the evening, going back home from work on the bus, people looked tired and had red-rimmed eyes from lack of sleep. When the alarm sounded as daylight faded, they looked at each other with a tired smile. There was a hint of sadness in that smile.

People who had no compelling reason to leave just stayed on. Staying in London was a sign of solidarity, a way of showing the unshakable will to resist. The children had been evacuated in good time and this was a great comfort. In the boarding house we used to go as usual, after dinner, into the large kitchen under the blacked-out glass roof to play darts. This was our challenge to the enemy and we stuck to it religiously, following the lead of the butler-cum-waiter and jack-of-all-trades of the boarding house, who always remained imperturbable, even when he set to work one night to extinguish the fire bombs which had fallen on our roof. Observing the perfect calm and method with which he quelled the flaming, spurting, evil things, one would think he had been doing nothing else all his life. James was a middle-aged Scotsman and a first-class darts player. He got the bull's-eye each time with the utmost ease and then double to finish the game on the first or second turn.

At night, most of the boarding-house guests went down to the basement during air raids. Some more apprehensive lodgers took refuge in the underground station a few blocks away. In the morning we used to go out to see the damage of the night's incursion. Some houses in the vicinity were just a mass of smoking ruins. A building about a hundred yards away from our boarding house was still standing as if by miracle. A bomb had fallen on it obliquely and destroyed the lower storeys and the greater part of the basement. Supported on just the thin outer brick wall, most of the third floor was still intact. The old lady who lived on that floor had decided to stay in bed during the air raid instead of going for protection to the basement. She was hale and hearty as the firemen saved her from that uncomfortable situation. I thought this was a presage that confirmed our ineffable James's often quoted saying: "They'd only get an old bird like her if the bomb had her name on it." We continued to play darts after dinner, under the glass roof, trying to show some of James's imperturbability.

The months followed each other and the bombing was getting heavier every night. I was anguished by the thought of having to leave my mother and my wife in this hell when the time came to join up. Some very close friends of ours, Jacques and Lisa Yael, former neighbours in Milan, had come to live in England many years before. Their home was in Manchester but they had evacuated to a small seaside resort on the West Coast as they had two little girls, Leila and Yvonne. They had asked us to come and live with them as soon as we arrived in England but we did not want to weigh on them. I now finally realised that the only solution was to leave my mother and my wife with them for the duration of the war. They had always said they had plenty of room for us.

We left our boarding house early one morning at the beginning of November. The bombing that night had been very heavy and many roads were closed to traffic. We had to take a train from Euston Station. As we arrived under the covered passageway where the taxis drew up, we became aware of an unusual state of confusion and entering the main concourse we found ourselves in the middle of an excited crowd, which was rushing from one platform to another. Loudspeakers were blaring all the time: "Trains will not be leaving from this station."

We heard that many railway lines had been uprooted by the night's bombing and were being repaired. We decided to wait at the station and huddled in a corner sitting on our luggage. Long hours passed. We had given up our rooms at the boarding house that morning. There had been people who were waiting to move in, so we could not go back there. We were at a loss, not knowing where we would spend the night. Daylight was fading and there was no more hope of leaving. We left our suitcases in the luggage room and joined the long taxi queue fearing, as night was falling, to hear the air-raid alarm go off at any moment.

Having finally got into a taxi, we started our long search for a place to spend the night. In the end we found accommodation in a large hotel in Regent Street. That night the fires of hell were let loose. The bombing, heavier than on previous nights, lasted till the first light of day. At midnight one of the hotel wings was hit and destroyed. Many people were killed. We left as soon as the all-clear was sounded. The havoc was still considerable. There were flaming buildings, an acrid smell of burning, thick smoke and masses of rubble blocking the streets. Ambulance bells were ringing all the time.

As soon as we got out of the taxi at Euston we heard the loudspeakers announcing that trains would not be leaving the station. The air-raid alarm was on again and bombs were still falling on the sidings. We recovered our suitcases and squatted in a corner again. The loudspeakers continued all the time. It was getting on towards midday. All of a sudden we heard over the loudspeakers that a train was leaving for our destination. We rushed to the platform that had been announced and got into one of the carriages. We had hardly sat down, breathless and worn out, when the loudspeakers croaked again, "Would all passengers alight. This train will no longer depart."

As we got up to leave, the train started to move very slowly. My wife and I could have easily jumped down, but my mother could not possibly have done it. We returned to our seats. The train was now proceeding in jerks, forwards and backwards. Accelerating for a while, it changed tracks and then went back six or seven times. We were waiting for it to stop definitively to enable us to get off, when the forward motion continued longer than before and the train started to move faster and faster. The rhythm of the wheels on the track became regular. We were off.

It seemed very strange to me that there were no people about in our carriage. I went scouting. The whole train was empty of passengers except for two railway guards who were brewing tea in a small service compartment. We arrived at St Annes-on-Sea at about four o'clock in the afternoon. As we got off the train it seemed to us we were entering a different world. We breathed peace and serenity in this corner of England that seemed so faraway from war and destruction.

Our friends had a large two-storey house with a garden, a vegetable patch and a hen-coop. They were very dear people and we soon found ourselves relaxing with them as part of one family. The images of London and the turmoil of war grew fainter in our minds as we adjusted to rhythms of daily life that seemed to have changed very little in this quiet little town. Old gentlemen still played their usual doubles matches on the Council tennis courts every day and their wives still sat in front of the beach (the sea looked very far off) and knitted tirelessly. One difference, I think, was the colour of the wool, which was now khaki or Air Force blue.

My wife and I went for long bicycle rides. The autumnal countryside was very beautiful. There were very few people about. We felt we were on a sort of holiday and banned all thoughts about tomorrow. My mother was also much happier having rediscovered some of her former habits and a new home with our friends.

Six weeks went past and then one morning the postman handed me a buff envelope stamped with the royal crest. It was marked on "His Majesty's

Service". After waiting for more than six months I had been called to duty. I was requested to report to a military training camp of the East Lancashire Regiment at Squire's Gate, only a few miles away from St Anne's, on the way to Blackpool. Was it the hand of providence or the benevolence of an intelligence Corps Depot Movement officer, as yet unhardened by military insensibility? For my preliminary training period I had been detached to that infantry regiment.

Before taking service I had to report to the Provincial District Officer, about twelve miles away from St Annes to take my oath. I took a train there the next day. The recruiting office was situated in a massive dark stone building not far from the station. There was a strong smell of disinfectant as one entered the premises. The ground floor was crowded with half undressed young men who went in and out of a door marked "M.O.". At a table near the entrance sat an old man in a blue siren suit. He had a small bar of multicoloured ribbons on his chest. I showed him my orders.

He looked at the paper for a while and then gave me a knowing wink. "Upstairs, first door, left," he said, moving his head in the direction of the stairs.

I went into a large room divided in the middle by a dark, wooden desk-like partition. Behind it sat three middle-aged gentlemen, at their working tables. As I arrived one of them got up and came towards me. He looked about sixty, tall and thin with chiselled features and greying hair. This distinguished man reminded me of a university professor or a judge.

I said "Good morning", and handed him my paper over the wooden partition. He greeted me civilly and started to read with attention the letter I had received from the Intelligence Corps. Without any comment he went to his table, picked up a form and started to fill it in front of me, on the high desk. At a certain moment, he stopped writing and said in a somewhat surprised voice, "You were born in Constantinople."

He lifted his eyes from the form he was filling in and looked at me steadily for a moment. When he had finished writing he said to me, "We must now proceed to the oath. What is your religion?"

"I am Jewish," I said.

"In that case," he added, "you have to swear on the Old Testament."

He moved a book with black covers towards me, which was on the bench nearby, and said again, "Put your hat on, please. Place your hand on the Bible and repeat with me."

I swore to serve and defend the King and the Nation faithfully until I was released, at the King's pleasure. I thanked the magistrate, for that seemed to be the old gentleman's function, and was preparing to leave when he put his hand on my arm, which was resting on the desk.

Looking at me intently, he said: "I wish to tell you my personal feelings about the oath you have just taken and ease a doubt which might disturb your conscience. I regard you as a loyal subject of the nation since you are volunteering for service and I believe that, in the same way, you would be loyal to your people under any circumstances. It is my firm belief that you will never be asked, in your service, to act against your kin, as such, except of course as the subjects of enemy nations."

This just man had foreseen the painful dilemma that would arise in the conscience of a Jew, constrained by circumstances to act against his own people, in their struggle to establish their homeland in Palestine. And I often had cause to remember this wise man's prediction in the various assignments I had to fulfil during my service: my superior officers took care every time that I did not have to face such a dilemma.

I took leave from this gentleman and went down for the medical examination. It was quite cold in the large hall, where we had to undress before entering one of the cubicles that lined the large space, in order to be vetted by the medical officer. The young recruits, mostly country boys and factory-hands from the Lancashire mills, all stood completely naked, waiting to be examined, jumping from one foot to the other. They laughed and joked all the time, and strangely, being naked as they were, I felt as one with these youngsters, who were yet so different from me. After the medical examination I was told to report to the Paying Officer who gave me my first pay to confirm that I was now irrevocably at the King's service. I took the train back home.

I had to report to camp the next day. I felt satisfied and at peace with myself. I had complied with the wish that was so near to my heart. The bus left me in front of the guard-house at the military training camp. It was a large area surrounded by a low wall and barbed-wire obstacles. It had previously belonged to holiday camp organisation. There were a few hundred bungalows, in perfect rows in the background, and various large brick and masonry compounds near the entrance.

I presented myself to one of the military policemen at the gate and was taken to the guard-room where a young corporal took me in charge. He must have been sixteen or seventeen years old. A drummer boy in the Indian army, as I learned later, he was treating me with a paternal solicitude which amused me very much. We proceeded to the equipment store to draw my uniform. I joined the queue. In front of me were many of the young lads I had met at the Recruiting Office having their medical examination. Looking at them as they were now, in sweaters, scarves, caps and heavy boots it struck me I had joined a different, but nonetheless, friendly world. As on the day before, there was a constant exchange of heavy jokes and loud laughter.

I had unearthed an old skiing outfit and a Norwegian cap at the bottom of a trunk we had brought from Italy. I thought these clothes would be more suitable to the occasion than a shirt and tie and sports jacket. Dressed as I was, I felt there was no danger of arousing the instinctive diffidence of these hearty young men for a carefully dressed unknown person. In the letter of instructions I had received from the Intelligence Corps, I had been told to take some pyjamas and a hairbrush with me to the camp. I never used pyjamas. My comrades slept in their underwear and so did I. As for the hairbrush, in the end we were issued with all the necessary brushes to keep us spick and span.

My turn came to draw my military outfit. I had already noticed the enraptured expression on the face of the recruits at the sight of the abundance of clothing that was lavished on them. I suppose that the majority of these unsophisticated lads had never possessed such a profusion of clothing all at one time. There were three long-sleeved woollen jerseys; singlets and long underpants; three woollen khaki shirts; three pairs of finger-thick soft woollen socks; two pairs of indestructible army boots, a uniform and heavy overcoat; fatigue denims; cotton singlets and shorts for gym, as well as plimsolls; towels; brushes of all kinds; a small brass, hinged tool to clean one's buttons without staining the uniform; black shoe polish; spare laces; a "housewife", a small cotton-tissue envelope containing needles and thread, small scissors and spare underwear buttons; a small first-aid kit; a haversack; a shoulder pack and a shiny mess tin. It was no joke carrying all this stuff away and many of the lads had to stop repeatedly to pick up what they had dropped on the way.

Four men were assigned to one bungalow. There were two iron bedsteads against each side of the hut with three thick woollen blankets on top of them. As we were walking to our bungalow we passed an open storehouse full of spring mattresses, which had been probably been left by the former holiday camp organisation. My companions gave a shout of joy at this sight and after throwing their mass of equipment on their beds, rushed to the storehouse and came back with a mattress each on their backs. I wasted no time in doing likewise. I was learning.

My three companions were all Lancashire lads, free of tongue and spontaneously friendly. We soon became friends. They were genuine persons with no frills about them. The salt of the earth. I felt I was something of a curiosity to my fellow soldiers. Who was this strange soldier who spoke English without any country inflection, who knew so many languages, drank less beer than they did at the pub, and did not relish cold tripe and vinegar at supper, which for most of them was a rare delicacy. I was without doubt quite a different sort of person, but this did not seem to hinder them, in the least, and they treated me as one of them. As time went on, I began to be regarded as a sort of oracle by my nearest comrades. I was consulted on all sorts of matters. In their eyes I was someone who knew everything. They even came to me to help them write their letters home.

I slept very well that first night on the spring mattress. It was bitterly cold. We were in December and the wind from the sea blew icily through the many cracks in our hut. The blankets kept me quite warm and my wife had knitted me a balaclava helmet of thick wool. As a result I had only a little frozen mucus under my nose in the morning. The sound of a bugle woke me up at about dawn. In my drowsiness I did not immediately realise where I was. At the double, we rushed to the washroom, which was under a corrugated sheet iron roof near by. There were some showers attached to it. The latrines were further away. Very rudimentary, they consisted in an empty oil drum with a rough wooden seat on the top. The problem was there were no doors to the cubicles where the drums stood. There was not a lot of privacy in this sort of arrangement but privacy was one of those things you soon forgot about in military life.

Breakfast was good and plentiful. Sitting at long tables, we passed our mess tins along to the front for tea and received a metal plate handed to us by the WRACs (Women's Royal Army Corps) with porridge, bacon or sausages. I noticed that some smart bloke slid a plate on his knees while lunging for another one. This sort of thing did not last long. The spirit of comradeship soon overcame such behaviour. The draft recruits were not all saints. There were some who in life had strayed from the path of righteousness. They were too smart and unscrupulous but they often turned out to be good comrades who taught many of us to get out of a difficult situation. A few days after joining the camp, our sergeant informed us there would be an equipment inspection by our company commander the next day. I was looking in vain for the second pair of boots with which I had been issued. They had disappeared mysteriously; I was in trouble. The drummer boy corporal who had taken me under his wing helped me out of this situation.

"Don't worry," he said, "I'll get you another pair."

Shortly after, he appeared with another pair of boots. I suppose that some other artless recruit, not belonging to our platoon, found himself without his second pair of boots on inspection.

We drilled hard during the whole day and went often for long marches in the countryside, burdened with full packs and rifle, in all kinds of weather. We were exhausted by the evening. We were learning how to use our weapons, how to shoot and use a bayonet. In the beginning I did not relish plunging my bayonet into a straw sack, running madly forward with a savage howl, but I confess that, after a while, I found a sort of satisfaction in doing this.

The first three months went by. On Sundays I had leave to go home. I had to be back in the evening. I noticed that our officers treated me with an unusual kind of regard and thought that this was due to the fact that I was a bit of a foreigner, somewhat different from the others. When I came back to visit the regiment after my promotion to second lieutenant I discovered the reason for their attitude. The young lieutenant who was in charge of my platoon said to me: "You thought we did not know you had been planted in this camp by the Intelligence Corps, to find out if our security measures were adequate?" I did not answer. I just smiled. I had learned a lot in the army, besides the use of weapons.

As my period of instruction at the camp was nearing its end I got into the habit of climbing over the wall at night, sometimes, to go and sleep home. I came back the same way in the very early morning. I was crossing the parade grounds one day, when I noticed the regimental sergeant-major, the most awe-inspiring military authority, dreaded by officers as well as by the troops, coming towards me. I stopped on the spot, rigidly at attention in front of him.

He transfixed me with a stern look and, addressing me in that icy voice which gave the whole regiment the shivers, said, without changing the expression on his face: "Beautiful moonlight, last night, on the wall, wasn't it, corporal?"

He turned on his heel, impeccably, and continued on his way accompanying his perfect regulation marching pace with his silver-topped cane, the emblem of his exalted position.

My training period was soon over. Four months had elapsed since my enlistment. It had been a happy period for me. I was given the opportunity to get to know the men who were the backbone of Great Britain, sound, headstrong, duty-conscious people, even when they joked about army discipline, with which they complied faithfully. I had integrated myself very well with my comrades. Although I had not been born in the country, I had been deeply influenced by the education I had received at the English school I had attended, in Constantinople, from the age of twelve until I was eighteen. I had been moulded into the British way of thinking and behaving by my teachers and by daily contact with many of my schoolmates, born in Great Britain, who were the sons of company managers of British firms that had opened offices in Turkey or of consular officers. Those young boys had not changed their habits and mentality in the least because of being in different surroundings and I had been ready to conform to their ways. I had learned to appreciate and react spontaneously to their dry humour, and with time I had discovered that cricket was not a tedious game. Above all, I had learned to distinguish between things that could and had to be done and those that were not in the book. I also trained myself to keep calm when my Mediterranean blood was attaining boiling point.

As a result of this education and mentality, it was England which became the environment that was most suited to my nature. I found myself very much at ease with my fellow soldiers. In the end it was like a repetition of my schooldays in different circumstances. After a few weeks in camp I learned to react like my comrades to the daily problems that presented themselves and not to cut a poor figure for being different. I tried to drink as much beer as they did at the pub, at the risk of bursting my bladder. I did my best to express myself like a native of Lancashire, so as to avoid being immediately asked, "And where do you come from, mate?" whenever we met troops from other regiments.

Six weeks after putting on my uniform I felt as if I had worn it all my life. It had been hard at first to try and look like real soldiers. As time went on, and following the example of the noncommissioned officers, most of them regular army soldiers, we got into the habit of pressing our trousers under the mattress, wearing our caps at the correct angle and polishing the top of our boots to shine like mirrors. I think that at that stage few of my companions had any nostalgic feeling about their former civilian life. Military service in times of war, even for the most cynical person, has a definite ennobling influence. In the struggle for existence, man generally finds himself alone and now being part of a group, which provides support and comradeship, he feels he is fighting a hard battle which has a wider scope than his personal problems, since it concerns the survival of his nation.

One day, our platoon sergeant, a good-natured country lad who took his stripes very seriously and tried to look gruff without success, came to our mess to inform us that there would be a boxing tournament among the troop. Entry was open to anyone except professional boxers. Quite a few soldiers put their hands up and I found myself too, with a raised hand. The sergeant was rather surprised that I, of all people, should wish to get myself punched about in the ring. I liked boxing. I had started doing it at school and used to patronise a small gym in Milan, in Via Santa Marta, where a former good welterweight named Zambon held a boxing academy. He had been in the foreground for a time and had finally resigned himself to managing the small, stuffy establishment that reeked of sweat and Scott's emulsion.

The contest was held. Most of the entrants, tough and courageous lads, had very little knowledge of boxing. I got easily through to the quarter-finals. Now came the more difficult part. I was only a heavy cruiserweight at 178 pounds and the last matches had to be fought against heavyweights as well. My opponent was a kind of giant. Twenty-four years of age, six-foot-four tall with heavy muscles, he was a baker by profession. He weighed 226 pounds. The young man was not very proficient but he had two very long arms and a terrific wallop. I was trying to control his youthful impetus when I took one of his very hard punches on the jaw (I could not chew for a fortnight after that). In general I never had a desire to maul my partners when boxing. They were usually friends of mine against whom I never had any grudge. Boxing was a rough sport all the same and one could get hurt at times.

Under the sting of that tremendous punch I felt my blood turn cold with a suppressed rage that I never thought I could have felt. With deadly intent I was now concentrating on finding an opening through my opponent's long arms and finally landed a straight punch to his heart, in which I had put all my weight and my desire to hurt the poor fellow. He fell like a sack and I was overwhelmed with a sentiment of joy, a wild primeval instinct that made me feel superior and powerful. I was shaken on later consideration, to have discovered in myself an animal, ferocious strain, which as a civilised being, I thought I could quell in my nature.

My comrades were overjoyed that their refined bungalowmate could use his hands to the point of knocking out a 226-lb giant, as well as being able to speak so many languages and to sing like an Italian tenor, something of which they were very proud. I suddenly became very popular and officers of other companies became aware of my unusual presence in camp.

The unfortunate young baker had lost his senses for some minutes and was very shaken by that merciless punch. I went to see him with a bandage around my jaw. I felt sorry for him but the wallop I had taken was definitely nothing to joke about. The next day I had to take my bandage off. I was in the ring for the semi-finals. My adversary was quite a fellow. As tough as nails, quick on his feet, he boxed like a professional. It did not last long and I was sitting on the floor dizzy with a hail of hard punches to the head that left me groggy. The lieutenant who was refereeing the match came to tell me that I could ask for my opponent's disqualification if I wished because I had received a last hit when I was almost on the floor. I thanked him but said it would not be fair to my rival since he was miles better than me and deserved his victory. As a matter of fact he was the final winner of the contest. I had to be satisfied with a bronze medal, which I keep as a precious memento.

We used to talk a lot, my bungalow comrades and I. One of them was a tall, powerful fellow whose hands looked as big as shovels. He was quiet and well-behaved, expressed himself with ease and knew everything about sports and home politics. I asked him one day what he did in civilian life and how much he earned. He said to me, "I'm a bricklayer's mate and earn five pounds a week. I give two pounds to my wife, one pound goes for the rent and thirty shillings I keep for beer and the dogs. Ten shillings we put on the side."

I asked him again, "Don't you wish you could earn more money?"

"No hurry," he said. "I'll be a master bricklayer in two years' time and earn twenty-five shillings more every week. That's plenty enough."

I always wondered at how satisfied my fellow soldiers seemed with their working condition. It is true that at that time the struggle for better wages was not very acute, but it seemed to me these people were quite satisfied with their way of life.

My other two comrades were, respectively, a street sweeper and a plumber. They had perfect table manners and kept themselves neat and orderly in all circumstances. The plumber was a jolly fellow, a bit on the fat side. He drew amusing caricatures and drummed quite well on the piano when we went to the pub.

"You, who are a Jew," he said to me, when we got to be more friendly, "could perhaps solve a mystery which has worried me for some time. I had a Jewish mate in civvy street working with me under a master. He was older than I and left the job a year and a half ago to work on his own. Now he's got a plumber's shop. Can you explain to me where he got the three hundred quid to start his business?"

"Now then," I said trying to look as wise as he thought I was, "how many years had you been working together?"

"Over five."

"How much did you earn a week?"

"Oh," he said, "the pay was really very good. We got six pounds from the owner and then there were the tips."

"Tell me," I asked my friend, "how much do you spend on beer every week?"

His rubicund face lit up with pleasure. "I drink a lot of beer, you know. Let's say thirty shillings or two pounds. It all goes."

"Look," I said, "did your mate drink as much beer as you did?"

"Not on your life! Beer did not go well with him. It upset his stomach. His beer money remained in his pocket all right."

"Can you reckon how much thirty shillings per week, for fifty-two weeks, for five years amounts to?"

My plumber friend burst out laughing. "Crikey," he said, "I got it now. That's the secret."

"Tell me," I said again, hoping to push my advantage still further, "do you still see your mate sometimes?"

"Of course I do, he lives round the corner from my house and we go to the pub together when I'm on leave. He drinks quite a bit now, you know. Beer doesn't upset his stomach any more."

We both laughed our heads off for a while.

The war was not going too well in these winter months of 1941–2. Great Britain was all on its own fighting against a victorious and all-powerful Germany, which nothing seemed to be able to curb. Invasion of our country was in the air. Weapons were still in short supply. There were just three Bren guns allotted to our company and these were taken to bits and remounted ten times a day, for instruction. I do not know how much service they would have offered if we had had to use them against the enemy when we manned the beaches in the vicinity of our camp at night. In total darkness, exposed to the icy wind, time never seemed to go by on sentry duty. After a while one imagined German paratroopers or black-faced commandos emerging suddenly out of dark corners. We tried to keep in good spirits and the will to resist never faltered, but many of us thought at night about the bombs which continued to fall on the cities where we had our cherished friends.

My training period at the East Lancashire Regiment camp came to an end. I had orders to proceed to the Intelligence Corps Depot at Winchester for further instruction. The moment had come to take leave from my comrades. I had grown very attached to these good fellows. We were going different ways. We would not have faced the dangers of war together and this thought now made me feel alone and weaker. At the moment of parting from one's comrades, emotion surges from its hiding and the fear of death creeps stealthily up from the dark corner of the mind where it has been suppressed. It is a fear that is always present, in one's subconscious, but it is more easily kept dormant when one is surrounded by others. We wished each other good luck. Some eyes were shiny. We all knew we would not meet again. I was leaving behind an important moment of my life. A stage in which it was only possible to look forward, having shed all former links with the habits and the conditions of the past, which one tried to erase completely from the mind lest they weaken one's purpose. Burdened like a mule I took the bus home to St Annes. I had three days' leave before reporting to Winchester where my actual inception into the Intelligence Corps was to take place.

In order to reach Winchester in the morning I had to spend a night in London and I decided I would go to my friend's house, the schoolmate with whom I had gone to work on arriving in London. I reached

London as it was getting dark. There was, as usual, a long taxi queue at the station and when my turn finally arrived, I noticed that a full colonel, bedecked with red tabs, was waiting behind me. He had a pair of very military-looking grey whiskers and a rather gruff appearance. I made a move to fall back and give him precedence. I should never have done so. The awe-inspiring personage gave me a withering look and said, "Now, get on with it, corporal. Don't dawdle." As I sat in the taxi trying to get over the sharp reproof, I was overwhelmed with pride and gratitude for the nation where a corporal does not lose his turn in a taxi queue in front of a full colonel.

I spent the night in the anti-aircraft shelter of the large building where my friend lived. The bombing lasted till dawn. The city looked a shambles when I took the train early in the morning. It would have been patched up during the day only to be turned again at night into the usual battlefield. As I looked out of the window, on the train that was taking me to Winchester through an unreal landscape of tilled fields, untouched woods, sleepy villages and small townships with intact roofs, it seemed almost incredible that I had left the ruins and havoc in London such a short distance away.

The Intelligence Corps Training Depot in Winchester was situated in one of those colleges in which young men of good breeding were prepared to enter university at Oxford or Cambridge. King Alfred's College was a monumental building, which sat on a sort of embankment halfway down from the top of the old town. Winchester had retained much of its medieval appearance, with a series of porticos with small old-fashioned shops, which seemed to have been there all the time. Entering the precincts of the college through a wide portal, I made my way along a wide alley, bordered by tall ancestral trees, where a squad of corporals was being drilled at the stentorian command of a stalwart sergeant, who seemed to have been cut out from an enrolment poster. As I discovered later, the military instruction of the corps was entrusted to a group of sergeant-majors detached from the Royal Guards regiments. These tough, uncompromising, professional men were meant to transform into real soldiers the heterogeneous specimens of human society, which formed the substance of the Intelligence Corps personnel.

There was a bit of everything in this crucible. University professors and company directors of British firms from all over the world; tea planters from India and Ceylon, and rubber plantation managers from Malaysia; high-society playboys and hard-bitten adventures; bespectacled experts in Oriental languages and archaeology lecturers. There were men over forty accustomed to facing difficulties of every kind and to command, as well as athletic young students full of warlike fervour. The atmosphere was totally different to that of the East Lancashire Regiment and my simple and genuine country boys and small town happy-go-lucky comrades.

Here the mood was of seething personal initiative, which the sergeant-majors of the Guards regiments tried to curb as much as possible by subjecting these refined, and often haughty, gentlemen to the most irritating chores of military life. In the morning, as a rule, the roll-call used to follow the same set pattern.

The sergeant-major in charge would ask, "Who speaks five languages?"

A few unwary newcomers would raise their hands.

"Good, since you speak so many, you can clean latrines this morning."

Sergeant-major: "Who speaks four languages?"

The hands of some imprudent young men would again shoot up.

"You, gentlemen, will go to the kitchen to wash dishes and peel potatoes."

Then, at the end, with less military gruffness, the sergeant-major would ask, "Any of you play some music?"

Thinking the danger definitely over now, some amateur concert players would come forward.

"Good, gentlemen, since I see there are four of you, you will kindly carry the piano from the gym to the assembly hall."

We slept in a large hall on bunk beds fashioned with rough wooden planks. The mattresses were canvas sacks filled with straw, which we had to replenish very often, as they sagged very quickly under our weight. As luck would have it, the fellow who slept in the lower berth of my bunk bed had also lived in Milan since his early youth. His father had gone to Italy at the beginning of the century. He had been sent to school in England and was now on the board of a large enterprise that distributed sewing machines in Italy. We lost sight of each other after Winchester but met again and resumed our friendship after the war, in Milan.

Our days were exhausting. As an alternative to the mental effort of absorbing the knowledge inherent to our particular duties, we were subjected daily to various demanding physical activities. We practised unarmed combat (the method of disposing of one's enemy without weapons did not go under the appellation of karate in those days). We went to the shooting range for revolver practice. We were taught the use and the handling of explosives and were trained intensively in the art of riding motorcycles like stuntmen.

I sincerely hated these motorcycle exercises, which were very similar to motocross contests nowadays. The rickety contraption, with which it was invariably my luck to be issued, used to snuff out just as I was reaching the top of the steep hill which we had to climb, and sliding backwards I was usually propelled into the dust. The real trouble was I had to push the heavy monster up the hill again with my heart coming out of my mouth. It was very important in our Field Security units to know how to handle a motorcycle in all circumstances. These special sections of the Intelligence Corps advanced with the frontline units and had to reach the enemy positions as soon as these were abandoned by them.

Soldiers were in the habit of pocketing small objects as war mementos, but to the Intelligence Corps these were very useful means of building up a general view of the German army and served to enlarge our knowledge. It was important to collect battle orders, as well as regimental tabs and buttons in order to ascertain which units were in the field. Letters received by dead soldiers could also offer useful information about the results of Allied bombing of targets of military importance in their home towns. We already had an extensive picture of the German army organisation and this formed a conspicuous part of the information imparted to us during our courses, which had to be memorised.

The Intelligence Corps personnel who were finally promoted to the rank of lieutenant and captain were detached to army corps and went into action as Information Officers. They were normally part of the General Staff. One learned quite a lot of things by attending, at various levels, the courses of the Intelligence Corps. Towards the end of our period of instruction we were transferred to Matlock, in Derbyshire, for the last and most exacting period of our training.

Matlock was a spa resort whose heyday had been during the first decades of the century. We were billeted in one of the monumental hotels built to satisfy the fashion for luxury and grandeur of the period. Its sumptuous bathrooms now offered us

Chapter Four

some of the comforts we had long forgotten. We were put under pressure throughout the day. The mental strain was very heavy. Towards the end of the course we were subjected to a war exercise designed to test our reactions under battle conditions. We had to carry on with our duties under the stress of loud bangs, rifle fire and machine-gun rattle, not to mention lack of water and food, and we were expected to solve confused and contradictory orders delivered by bemused motorcycle orderlies.

The course at Matlock lasted four weeks. I became acquainted with Bass No. 1 beer, an exquisite poison that knocked you out after a couple of pints. I also got to know an Irish girl who acted as a ticket collector on the local bus. She was fair and easy to get on with. She also liked to talk and danced very willingly with soldiers. I also noticed she listened very attentively. It did not take long, for my comrades and myself, fresh as we were from our courses on enemy spying methods, to understand the reason of her interest in our conversation and, after some close watching, to uncover the spy ring of which she was a member. She was taken into custody together with an accomplice, the telephone operator at the hotel where our staff were billeted, who had certainly heard more than she should.

We went back to Winchester and got ready to embark for the African Front. We had already been issued with our summer overseas kit and were waiting to leave any day when I woke up one morning with severe pains in the lower part of my abdomen.

I realised I was suffering from an attack of kidney stones, since I had already suffered the same excruciating pain during the bombing in London one night. The doctor who assisted me then had told me, after examining my x-rays, that there was no need for an operation right away, but that I should have the calculus out if the ailment recurred. I was taken to a large hospital a few miles out from Winchester. As I was lying in the ambulance, I felt I would be separated again from my new comrades. They would leave without me and I would be on my own, yet another time.

A year and a half had passed and I was stationed in Cairo. As I was returning to my lodgings in town one evening, dizzy with heat and overwork, I bumped into a sergeant who had stumbled on the uneven pavement. We looked at each other and than a flash of recognition lit our faces. He was one of my comrades from the Winchester group, which had left for Africa when I was taken to hospital.

He told me the story of our Field Security section on its first mission into the desert. On returning to base there were only five men left. Seven out of the twelve components of the group were missing, including the lieutenant in command. They were prisoners or dead, no one seemed to know.

At the hospital in Winchester I had to undergo various tests. The calculus was there all right, but deeply embedded in the urethra. It was very small and difficult to extract. I was released for a time, with instructions to drink twelve pints of water a day and skip with a rope for all I was worth. I had to report to hospital periodically. I often suffered severe pain but it did not last long. During that time I was attached to the Field Security section in Winchester. I could not be transferred overseas because if it had become necessary to operate on me urgently, I would have been an additional burden on the military hospitals in Cairo, which had enough work with the wounded on the African Front. In England, the situation in military hospitals was much easier and troops were operated on for latent hernia or possible appendicitis. To lengthen the casualty list at the hospital near Winchester, there was however a steady flow of broken arms and legs from the motorcycle training course at the Intelligence Corps Depot.

The activity of the Winchester section, which was billeted in an old house in the upper part of the town, consisted in checking the security measures of the troops dislocated in the neighbourhood. At night, we also often went on motorcycle patrols to Portsmouth or Southampton, when these ports were the target of air bombing raids, to ascertain whether lights were being flashed by enemy agents to pinpoint important sites.

One night, during an assignment, while the bombing was very heavy, my motorcycle broke down. I was always very awkward at handling these contraptions. This time, however, the flooded carburettor saved my life. The patrol's assembly point was in front of a large building a couple of hundred yards from where I had stopped. Suddenly there was a short whistling sound and a tremendous crash. The earth trembled under my feet. The bomb had fallen exactly on the spot where we would have met. Nobody was there yet. Not even I.

In and out of hospital I was finally detained for my operation. I was lucky because the surgeon was a Harley Street highlight. The calculus was so small it could hardly be located. The operation lasted a long time and the local aesthetic, which had been injected into the spine, was already waning when it was finally extracted. I was rather shaken and my condition remained critical for a few days. My wife was informed and I found her unexpectedly at my bedside. I had to stay in hospital much longer than I thought and was only granted home leave after spending a period of three weeks in a convalescent home at Henley-on-Thames.

I will always remember this heavenly spot. The mansion in which we were housed was in the middle of a beautiful park. From the bow window of the large room, where we sat after our meals, we could watch the deer and their fawns nibble the grass almost under our nose. We were ministered to by lovely, young, voluntary nurses belonging to the families of local residents. There were also some stern military nurses and an iron-fisted, disciplinarian matron. In the enervating atmosphere of this spot of paradise we were recovering, along with our health, the unrestrainable promptings of our youthful vitality.

After too short a period of home leave I returned to the training centre at Winchester. The place was deserted. My comrades had all gone a long time before. Another intake had been trained and transferred overseas and now a new batch of recruits was expected. I felt still rather weak and was certainly not in high spirits in this dismal atmosphere. The former squad of sergeant-majors from the Guards had been replaced by newcomers. There was only one sergeant I knew who was in charge at the canteen.

I was lolling one morning on one of the bunks of the empty dormitory, in prey to a particularly depressed mood, when I was suddenly confronted by the new regimental sergeant-major. He was a tall, well-built figure of a soldier. His stern expression was mitigated by his intelligent, deep-set eyes.

He looked at me severely: "Where do you think you are, corporal, on leave! Now get up, sharply, get hold of a broom and clean up this pigsty."

I got up immediately and did as I was told. Later that evening, I was sitting at a table in the canteen, in front of a glass of beer, which did not taste like much, when the regimental sergeant major came in. All ranks present sprang to attention.

"At ease," he said calmly and came towards me. "I'm sorry, corporal," he said, "I did not know you had just come back from home leave, after hospital. You will be on light duty from now on. You can take care of my own quarters."

He smiled kindly, said good evening and was off. We became very good friends. He was an intelligent and wise man with whom one could talk openly on serious arguments. He commanded respect and devotion from the troops for his sense of justice and his readiness to help them, instead of constraining them to blind military discipline. Keeping his quarters spick and span was a duty in which I took great pride.

I stayed at the training centre for a few weeks and having recovered strength was put back on active service again at the Winchester section and promoted to the rank of sergeant. I was in charge of the section's administration. However, I was dispensed from riding a motorcycle. The long scar on my abdomen would not have held the strain, in the hospital medical officer's opinion. This hindrance, I must admit, did not disturb me in the least. I definitely did not like motorcycles.

There were rumours about Turkey entering the war on our side and I applied for a commission thinking I would be more useful as an officer in such circumstances. A short time after I had returned on active service a despatch was forwarded to our office. I had to report as soon as possible to a very secret Intelligence unit not far from London.

I reported the next day and was interviewed by a major who explained to me, that in view of my knowledge of French as a mother tongue, I had been selected as a possible element to be parachuted into France to establish contact with the Resistance. I was given a test in French, which proved satisfactory. I would have to be put through an intensive parachute course at once.

As I was taking leave from the major, he asked me: "I take it you are graded A1, judging by your appearance."

"I'm sorry, Sir," I said, "I had an operation a few months ago and I am still graded B5. A scar on my abdomen is not completely healed yet."

The major frowned and his face darkened a bit. "Nothing doing, sergeant. We cannot drop you and have your wound reopen. You'd be no use. We'll talk about it in a few months."

I saluted and left the office. I confess I was not disappointed to be remanded. My stay in hospital and the period of poor health had weakened my spirit. Exciting as the assignment would have been, I dreaded the idea of facing danger on my own. I had become too gregarious and group-dependent. I went back to my section at Winchester. Some weeks went by and I was promoted to the rank of second lieutenant after a final interview with the colonel commanding the depot. I would now have to go through the Officers' Intelligence Course at Oxford.

I had never been to Oxford and was immediately affected by its particular atmosphere. We had our courses at Oriel College and I was billeted at Pembroke. The officers' course was more of an academy than a military institution. I met and made friends with the best elements suited for this job in the British Empire. It was like an intellectual convention on military science. The mental strain of keeping a wealth of important and secret information in mind was very taxing.

I came back to Winchester and some weeks later our group received instructions to be ready for embarkation. There was also a telegram from home. My mother was dying. She had lung cancer. I had known it for the last six months and dreaded I would be away from her at her deathbed. I went to see the adjutant.

He told me, "You are on the list to go any day, but perhaps you have time to see your mother. I'll give you three days' leave. In case you are wanted back immediately, I'll send you a telegram."

I found my mother had already died. Her weak heart had given up a few hours before I arrived. She had not suffered. We buried her in the cemetery at Blackpool. Poor mother, she had never got used to life in England and when we walked by the small graveyard in St Annes, not very far from where we lived, she frequently said, "I would not wish to be buried here, so far from everybody I know."

When I came back to Oxford my group was still there. Two days later there was a despatch for me from the High Command of the Intelligence Corps in London. I had to report to them, without delay. I was there the next morning.

"We want you to translate into Turkish a pamphlet about some very secret military information which can be only entrusted to Intelligence Corps personnel. Are you in a position to do it?"

I felt the sweat running down my back. The pamphlet was a manual about the disposal of German time bombs, which the British had learned to defuse, saving the lives of many bomb disposal men. I could not possibly translate the technical terms into Turkish. They did not exist even in the dictionary.

I asked the general, "At what level has this information to be divulged, Sir?"

He said, "It is destined for the use of the troops, from sergeant to captain. Colloquial language will do."

"In that case," I said, "I'll do my best!"

I felt I could do this by translating into common language the function of each of the complicated devices, which had no counterpart in the vernacular. I came back to Oxford with the precious booklet in the inside pocket of my tunic and started work on it at once. It took me almost two months to finish the job.

My Oxford course group left a few days after my return from London. It seemed I was always destined to be left behind by my comrades. Of all those who had finished the course with me at Oxford, I only met one after the war. He was an outstanding organist and I often accompanied him to the College chapel to listen to beautifully played Bach or Haydn.

It was not long before we heard that a substantial part of the convoy, which had left when I was held back at Oxford, had been torpedoed in the Atlantic Ocean. I went back to the High Command in

London to deliver the result of my work. I was admitted into the presence of a board of high-ranking officers and was asked point-blank if I did not wish to stay on at General Headquarters to attend to eventual assignments of this kind. I answered with due military deference that my desire was to re-join my comrades on active service overseas. When I told my wife, who had come to stay with me at Oxford, while I was busy attending to my translation, about the outcome of my interview in London, she proved again how exceptional a woman she was. She said to me: "You have done well to say you didn't want to stay in England. You would have been unhappy all your life for staying back. It's right you should go overseas."

The day arrived soon afterwards. I had to join the next convoy leaving from Glasgow. I said goodbye to my wife on the train platform at Oxford. Looking at her through the window, as the train was leaving the station, I saw she was standing erect looking fixedly in front of her as if she had been turned to stone.

Heavy squalls of rain were blurring the window-panes of the upper deck lounge of *S.S. Sibajak* as we were waiting to sail from Glasgow on that cold January morning. The dark mass of the tall vessels moored alongside shut out, almost completely from our sight, the dim outline of the city emerging from a greying fog. The officers belonging to the embarked troops were all gathered in the large, oblong room, sitting at small tables or lounging in the comfortable easy chairs ranged around the walls. Our last letters home, undated and with no indications as to where they had been written, had already been handed in to the mail orderly. The ship's destination was not known. There was little talk and a sense of expectation. Going away from England gave me the strange impression that I had completed a chapter in my life. The journey towards the unknown, perhaps with no return, did not cause me any anguish, pervaded as I was with a deep sense of fatality. A slight shudder went through the ship. Glasses and bottles tinkled on the tables. Slowly we started to move. It was as if all this was happening in a sort of dream.

The tall liner on which we were travelling offered a considerable measure of comfort since it had plied between the port of Rotterdam and Indonesia as a passenger and cargo ship in peacetime. The stewards on board were Malay. Small, dark men. They announced meals on a little harp, which had a very melodious, sweet sound. The ship's capacity was 18,000 tons. It had embarked two thousand men, field guns, ammunition and other material. The officers slept in the first- and second-class passenger cabins. The troops were quartered on the decks, at various levels and in some holds, which had been transformed into dormitories and mess rooms.

As I was not attached to any of the embarked regiments, I was granted privileged accommodation in a two-berth cabin on the first deck, which I shared with another officer who did not belong to any of the units on board. We all stayed in the lounge to have a drink after the ship's departure. The atmosphere had warmed up considerably. Loud guffaws were heard here and there. We had returned to the reality of our military condition, after having perhaps for a moment looked back with sad regret at what had to be left behind.

The weather cleared and now the sun shone brightly, high in the clear sky. On the dark green ocean, a swell of white-capped waves was breaking against the hulls of the multitude of ships, which dotted the water as far as the eye could see. Large cumbersome vessels filed one behind the other in the middle of the convoy, while the rest of the picturesque armada, made up of all kinds of floating hulks, hovered around. The progress was slow to keep pace with the smaller vessels. Three swift torpedo boats shot around and across the ponderous mass of shipping, turning sharply at right angles and lifting white transparent plumes of crystalline water in their wake. There were two cruisers in the distance. One was stationed at the back of the convoy, while the other, on the side but well in front, was sending continuous light signals to the torpedo boats.

It was freezing cold. The biting air dispersed the figments of a lingering ache in my benumbed mind. As the convoy left Glasgow, it headed towards the North Atlantic, hoping to avoid enemy submarines in the heavy seas that kept this stretch of ocean in turmoil at that time of the year. We were caught one night in a tremendous storm and were in great danger of sinking. It appeared that the holds of our ship were not full to capacity and that the cargo was not equally balanced. When the heavy seas hit the ship's flanks, it leaned over most dangerously. The furniture broke loose and crashed ominously against the sides of the ship and the glass and crockery in the dining-room pantry was broken to smithereens. Dismal creaking was heard when the boat leaned over and it felt like ages until it regained an even keel. It was lucky we did not capsize. The next day the ship's crew would not comment on the events of the previous night, but it was not difficult to conclude we had barely got away with it.

I had no special duties to attend to on the boat and was asked by the colonel in command of the troops to lecture the various units on security measures and acquaint them as much as possible with the characteristics of the enemy troops they would have to face on the battlefield. I went from one hold to the other and on various decks where the soldiers were quartered. On the upper decks where the officers had their cabins, the danger of being torpedoed seemed less frightening than in the lower portion of the ship, below water level, where there was no chance of escape if a torpedo had struck. I think that in spite of the show of high spirits and the cracking of the usual jokes in the soldiers' quarters, the same thought was in everybody's mind. However, it was also true that if anyone were to fall into the icy waters of the Atlantic, whether officers on the high decks or soldiers in the holds, there would be very little to be happy about. One would freeze to death in a few minutes. To keep the troops on their toes the alarm was sounded now and then, in a succession of blood-chilling, imperative toots. We rushed to the assigned spot on the bridge, in front of the lifeboats, with lifebelts correctly knotted. There were not as many lifeboats as we might have wished and it was much better not to reckon too carefully how many of us would have found room on these boats.

The weather was slowly getting better and the sea had turned almost calm. After calling at Lagos for a few hours, looking at it from the far end of the port as we could not disembark, we proceeded on our way to Cape Town. The ocean was now a beautiful boundless expanse of dark blue water. During the day we often saw nautilus shells, gliding by on the water, like diminutive sailing boats. Swarms of flying fish, like glistening silvery clouds, lifted themselves suddenly out of the water to land on the decks of our ship. At times, in the far distance we could distinguish vaporous jets soaring out of the water. Whales, we were told, but we could not see them.

At night we spent a long time on the bridge. In the total darkness, the vault of the sky was studded with a multitude of brilliant stars, which seemed so near we could touch them. A wide luminous wake of phosphorescent plankton followed the ship like the tail of a comet. The absolute darkness of the water merging with the starlit sky gave one the impression of travelling into space, a hypnotic sensation that annihilated all thought.

We crossed the Equator and there was a party on board ship. We were given a diploma by the captain. Everyone tried to keep in good spirits. Friends were easily made on the boat and groups were formed. My particular company included a young Cambridge university lecturer, who told us all about the stars at night, on the bridge, my cabin mate, a weathered Scotsman who explained to us how he ran his rubber plantation in Malaysia, a jolly Irishman always ready for a laugh or a fight, and the chief medical officer, a major. He was born in Manchester and had all the ready friendliness of the Lancashire people. He liked to tell us spicy jokes. His eyes shone with glee and he was the first to laugh about them. As he was telling them his round belly shook with happiness over his too-wide regulation army shorts.

One night he called us officially to council. There was a rather spiny problem to be solved and it needed serious discussion. We were nearing Cape Town and the matter was getting urgent. The query was whether the troops should or should not be issued with a set of French letters before disembarking in Cape Town. If this were not done there was danger of a spread of venereal disease when the soldiers came back from invading the low quarters of the port, disembarking after six weeks of continence. If, however, these instruments of licentiousness were foisted on the young warriors, such an official move might have been interpreted as an encouragement towards fornication. We pondered over the question and came to the conclusion not to issue the prophylactics. There lurks, in the dark corner of every British mind, an unforgotten biblical command, which always or nearly always comes to the fore. I still wonder at times, when this strange circumstance comes to my mind, where in heaven our medical officer would have found the thousands of rubber johnnies needed to provide two thousand lusty men with this protection. Was this war material, perchance, scored in the holds under the cases of ammunition?

We finally arrived in view of Cape Town. The sight of the lovely bay, shimmering with reflected light under the blue sky, and the massive unexpected shape of Table Mountain was a breathtaking spectacle. Swarms of small sailing boats were gliding, under full sail, over the water. The whole landscape breathed such an atmosphere of serenity that we felt we were landing in a completely different world. A realm of perennial summer, where the anguish of war was not known.

Disembarking, we were transferred to a transit camp, some five or six miles from the city, not far away from one of the most popular beaches in Cape Town. There was a small train that shuttled between the suburbs and the town. A row of benches stood at the end of the platform. Some were marked "For whites only". As soon as we had settled ourselves in our new quarters, we decided to go to town, and have some fun in a nightclub. We were soon informed that nightclubs in town were all run as private institutions. Officers could be admitted but drink was not provided. Club members had to bring their own bottles. We were rather crestfallen.

It was already six o'clock in the evening and liquor stores were all dutifully closed. We were wandering rather disconsolately through the almost deserted streets, not far away from the port area, when we noticed a swarthy, middle-aged, heavy-set character, his shirtsleeves rolled over his hairy, powerful forearms, taking the fresh evening air in front of his half-shuttered grocery store. I lifted my eyes to read the sign over the shop. My Mediterranean instinct had not led me astray. The man was Greek. I took a few steps and stood in front of him.

"Brother countryman," I said to him in the vernacular Greek my nanny had taught me, "could you not sell us a bottle of whisky, for God's mercy."

The good man's face lit up with a happy, incredulous smile. He could hardly believe that he was hearing the language of his native village from the mouth of a British officer in Cape Town. We got the bottle. As a matter of fact, we got two bottles of good whisky.

We had to wait for almost a month in Cape Town before we could embark for Egypt. There were no ships available. The large liner that had brought us from England had been torpedoed a few miles out of port on its way back. There were no troops on board and it appears the crew was saved almost to a man.

Waiting in South Africa was almost like a holiday. We forgot about the war and enjoyed the opportunity to see the surrounding countryside, travelling at times through the wild, luxuriant vegetation, which well epitomised the compelling lure of Africa. We were often invited by residents and treated with warm hospitality.

One night I was very late getting back to camp. There were no more trains and I was looking in vain for a taxi. I rang the bell at the door of a kind of motorcar-repair workshop. A light came on behind a window on the top floor of the garage and the curly head of a black man appeared suddenly. He had grey hair.

"Go away," he said none too gently. "This is no time to disturb honest people."

I addressed the man very politely and asked him if he knew where I could find a taxi to take me back to the camp. Unexpectedly his voice became very gentle. "I'm coming down, right away, Sir," he said.

Moments later, the door was opened and I could enter the workshop.

"You must excuse me," said the man with great dignity, expressing himself in good English. "I did not notice you were a British officer. I thought you were South African. I'll take you to camp. You are courteous and civil people. My son serves at table at your mess and tells me black people are treated like human beings and thanked for their service."

We spoke at length during the journey. He was a wise man and reasoned with great logic. I had a lot of trouble in getting him to accept the fare for the taxi ride.

On the day the regiment moved from the camp to leave for Egypt, the black waiters with their wives and children lined up along the roadside with all the village people. They were shouting, "God bless you and bring you safely back home."

Moored to the quay was a beautiful white ship. It was a Royal Navy auxiliary vessel, which was used in peacetime to transport troops to India. It looked like a luxury passenger liner and was equipped and designed with great practical sense and also to ensure reasonable comfort. We left a few hours after embarking. There was no mystery about our destination this time. We were going to Egypt.

We docked at Durban the next evening and stayed there for two days. The city was much less attractive than Cape Town and struck me as somewhat barren. I also recollect a particular negative image from Durban, one that has remained vividly in my mind all through these many years. It is perhaps less due to the fact that it was unusual than because it caused me some bitterness. As the ship was moored to the quay there was a long line of rickshaws waiting to take us for joy rides across the city. Prancing like horses the coolies dragging the rickshaws were gigantic black tribesmen adorned with long ostrich feathers stuck in their headdresses. The sight of these magnificent specimens of manhood galloping like horses for a few coins gave me a deep sense of humiliation.

We did not call at any port after Durban until we arrived at Port Tewfik on the Red Sea, at the mouth of the Suez Canal. The journey was extremely pleasant because of the beautiful weather and the clear nights but we had some excitement all the same. Twice during the night we had to jump from our beds as the alarm was sounded. It seemed there was a submarine giving us the chase. We had no escort of any kind. There were some depth bombs on the afterdeck and a gun here and there, but I don't think we would have stood any chance if things had taken a turn for the worse. Strange to say the idea of landing in the water here did not give me any qualms. The sea was not the icy whirlpool of the North Atlantic. It was as smooth as oil and gave one a great desire to swim in it.

We disembarked at Port Tewfik and proceeded by train to Cairo. The heat was overpowering. We stopped about six miles from the city to be directed towards a transit camp. That night we slept under a tent. We were in the middle of the desert and it got bitterly cold. It seemed incredible to suffer such an extraordinary low temperature after the tremendous heat of the day. I reported the next day to General Headquarters at Cairo to be informed about my further destination. My papers had not arrived yet.

On leaving England it had seemed probable that I would have been posted to Turkey, as a liaison officer with the Turkish army, if that nation had by then decided to come into the war on our side. But Turkey had decided in the meantime to remain neutral and I was at a loose end with no special assignment, which explained why no instructions had arrived as to my posting. I was annoyed to be left in mid-air. It is important in the army to be part of a definite group, to have comrades and to know one's final destination. The lieutenant in charge at headquarters handed me a form and said: "Since there are yet no definite orders for you, will you please fill in this form listing your particular qualifications and training and we will try to find somewhere to fit you in."

I completed the questionnaire mentioning the training I had undergone and the languages I knew. I had a vague fear I would be assigned to censorship. I handed the paper to the lieutenant. As he read its contents, his expression denoted an increasing interest. When he had finished reading he said to me with a great smile: "I think you've just been sent by heaven. We've a request that will fit you like a glove. Here's the address."

I took a taxi and arrived in front of a large villa, in the middle of a garden not far away from the Nile.

"Go up these stairs, Sir." said the orderly. "You will find the major in the room on top."

167

The large room was half in darkness. The blinds were down because of the heat. I stopped for a moment at the entrance to set my bearings. At the end of the room an officer was sitting at a desk, looking at some papers. I heard his voice before I could distinguish his features.

"Victor, you old son of a gun! What the hell are you doing here?"

I recognised him immediately. The major was a Scottish friend of mine who was one of the directors of an important textile industry in Milan. We used to spar together in the small gym in Via Santa Marta. This was indeed a fortunate encounter. The section under my friend's command was a part of the Political Intelligence Centre at the General Headquarters in Cairo.

Our work was regarded as extremely useful by the High Command. We were a separate unit and enjoyed considerable independence under our own officers. There were four of us under the authority of my friend, the major, and a dozen or so Intelligence Corps sergeants. The bulk of the section's personnel were all civilian. It was an interesting mix of men and women belonging to various Balkan and Mittel-European countries. Our small group of monitors was made up of Greeks, Bulgarians, Yugoslavs, Albanians, Turks, Romanians, German Jews, Italian anti-Fascists and Czechoslovak disbanded army officers. We also had some Jewish, so-called Palestinian personnel, who mostly belonged to units attached to the British army. One of them, a young Yugoslav, was a pioneer who had contributed to founding one of the first kibbutzim on Lake Tiberias, but he left our section to be dropped by parachute into Yugoslavia in order to help British pilots who were stranded there. Quite a few monitors were born in Egypt and belonged to the ethnic minorities scattered all over the Near East, but many of them had found refuge in Egypt after having had to abandon their native countries when they were invaded by the Nazis.

Day and night we listened to the Balkan countries under Nazi dominion, and to Romanian and German broadcasts as well as other radio stations, depending on the political necessities of the moment. The broadcasts were registered on wax cylinders to be later typewritten and translated. The particular function of the Intelligence officer was to distinguish, from among the mass of information and household topics broadcast by these stations, any elements of strategic or political importance that might have slipped through the meshes of the enemy censorship and which, collated with information obtained from other intelligence sources, could give us a clearer picture of the situation in these occupied countries.

The responsibility was a great mental strain. We could not allow any information to pass scrutiny, without sifting all its possible implications. It was imperative to be completely in the picture at all times, to know everything about the political situation in these countries, in order to be able to follow, day by day, the changes which could occur in the local administration, such as the defection of some official to the German authorities or the imposition of new restrictive measures. Power cuts caused by the lack of coal, much of which was sent to Germany, or increased food rationing due to the same reason were also indicative of the situation and the conditions of life in occupied Balkan countries and instrumental in establishing the degree to which the Germans needed these supplies in order to maintain their war effort. This information also served as groundwork for the propaganda leaflets that were scattered over these countries by our airplanes or distributed secretly among the population.

In compensation for our exacting work we were not subject to rigid army discipline and could swap our hours of duty among ourselves in order to enjoy some periods of leisure. Our section was a true microcosm. Among the monitors of various languages everyone had a long story to tell. There were refugees, political dissenters, dispersed military personnel from armies that no longer existed, and people from other parts of the world who had come to live in Cairo for one reason or another, brought there by the ups and downs of their particular lives.

I discovered in our section a Turkish friend of mine who had been a pupil of the English High School for Boys in Constantinople at the same time as I was. He had come to Cairo in the wake of the family of a former sultan who had been exiled to Egypt. In our German section there was an

Egyptologist known to everyone as Burchardt, who was a scion of the Warburg family. There was also the daughter of a German luminary of medicine who had emigrated to Turkey for racial reasons and was now head of the faculty of medicine in Istanbul. In general, they were all men and women who through this work wanted to do their share of fighting the common enemy.

The Intelligence Corps officers were all jolly good fellows, capable men who had spent most of their lives away from England, holding responsible jobs in foreign countries. Among my fellow officers one in particular stood out: he was a scholar, a Welshman, who knew fourteen languages and was still learning others. He knew Chinese, Sanskrit and Armenian among others. He was a gentle soul who lived in a world of his own, one in which his uniform had introduced no change whatsoever.

One day we became aware that the broadcasts to which we were listening regularly had become completely unintelligible or had faded out altogether. It was obvious that the Germans had cut the power of these broadcasts so as to reduce the likelihood that they could be heard outside the country in which they were transmitted. We had to find a way to overcome this situation. Such a possibility had already been foreseen and a PIC (Political Intelligence Centre) colonel had already gone to Turkey some time previously to study the possibility of continuing our monitoring system from Istanbul. Turkey, although neutral, had not prevented the Germans or the Americans from setting up listening systems based inside their embassies in the country. It was regarded, one might say, as a diplomatic privilege.

It was decided that I should to go to Istanbul to organise our section's work. I left Cairo in the autumn of 1943 and was seconded to the British Embassy in Turkey as a civil servant.

Chapter Five

The journey was to be made by train, travelling through Palestine and Syria. I had three days' leave and I decided to stop in Tel Aviv where my wife's brother had come to live at that time. Israel did not yet exist as a nation except in the hearts and minds of those resolute idealists who had emigrated to the country early in the century to bring their dream to reality. Some pioneers had come later and a few were allowed to land on its shores. However, the bulk of the Jewish population only managed to enter Palestine after untold difficulties and obstacles, a situation that deteriorated still further when swarms of destitute Jews fleeing from Nazi terror had no other alternative than to find refuge there or die.

I had never felt ill at ease in my Jewish skin. Moreover, I had never, fortunately, come into close contact with the rabid anti-Semitism to which Jews had been subjected in Russia, Poland and Romania, and later, with such demented fury, in Hitler's Germany.

As I walked through the streets of Tel Aviv I felt a sense of elation to be among people whom I felt close to at an atavistic level although so many of them were different to me in origin, language and custom. There was a basic sentiment of belonging that went very deep. I entered a small haberdashery in one of the side streets of the main thoroughfare. I needed a button for the jacket of the civilian suit I would have to wear when I left Palestine for Turkey. In my army uniform, with my peaked cap well down on my rosy occidental face, I did not think my Jewishness was evident. I asked the old lady in the shop, in English, if she could supply my needs. The woman, who was about sixty, and probably of Polish or Romanian origin, scrutinised me for a few moments and burst out in Yiddish:

"But you are Jewish, my dear captain, are you not?"

I was very proud of my uniform, very proud to serve the British Empire of which I considered myself a loyal subject, but the old lady's exclamation filled me with great joy. I suddenly felt a deep sense of kinship with her and through her friendly forwardness I became more acutely aware of what it meant to these poor, castaway, persecuted people to have found a haven. A country in which a Jew was always welcome and could be himself.

I arrived at Istanbul, having travelled for the last lap on a ferry, which took me there from İzmit on the Sea of Marmara. Eighteen years had gone by since I had left Turkey and save for a brief holiday, before the war, I had never returned. Around me I could hear the language of my youth.

An embassy representative was waiting for me at the quay and drove me to the hotel where I would be staying. It was already late in the evening and we went to dinner at one of the smart open-air restaurants in town. Not far away from our table I noticed a distinguished gentleman with greying hair dining with a group of people who were showing him great deference. It was Herr Von Papen. It gave me quite a turn to be confronted with one of the archenemies. Civilian clothes were a mitigating influence, but it took me some time to grow accustomed to living elbow-to-elbow with Germans and to seeing the Nazi flag flying over the German Embassy, plumb across the road from my in-laws' apartment windows.

Opposite to where I was sitting at dinner, I suddenly noticed a cousin of mine, at a table with her husband. When she saw me her face went white, as if she had seen a ghost. Knowing I was in the army she probably thought I was already dead. I gave her a sign to be silent and phoned her later to explain the situation.

Istanbul, like Lisbon, was a nerve centre for the activities of the secret services of all the nations involved in the war. Both sides had spies everywhere, especially among those people who seemed above suspicion. There were informers among the hotel and restaurant staff and the lower elements of the various ethnic minorities, but the most efficient agents were most likely to be camouflaged among the smart international set of diplomats and high-society elements. Information from the Nazi-occupied Balkan countries filtered through our services every day and had to be carefully analysed. The most complicated intrigues and subtle infiltrations were constantly changing and bluff and counterbluff were the order of the day. The game was not without danger and now and again somebody disappeared from the stage, in silence.

When I arrived at the end of the summer of 1943, Turkey was leaning strongly towards the Axis. The war at that moment seemed to tend towards the German armies and their success confirmed the warlike quality of their troops, certainly in the opinion of a large proportion of Turkish officers who had been trained in German military academies. However, British and Americans were still tolerated in Istanbul. Turkey was a neutral country and in every respect the Turks were very conscious of their national dignity, which they allowed no one to impair.

For us, on the other hand, it was quite difficult at that time not to give umbrage to our hosts. In our secret service at the embassy I had come into contact again with some of my schoolmates of British nationality who had remained in Turkey after I had left the country in 1926. The head of the service was a former pupil of my school in the years before 1914–18. He was a man of about fifty whom I admired very much. He had been a magnificent athlete and when I was at school after the First World

War, he was still in such good form as to win the Old Boys' hundred yards' race year after year at our annual school games.

The advantage of having been born in the country helped me very much to contact the people I wanted, without giving any due to enemy agents as to my purpose. German and Allied agents crossed and followed each other in the streets. The watch was constant and those who could not camouflage themselves among the city's inhabitants were easy to uncover and their moves became apparent. I knew everybody in town and could stop to talk with dozens of people in the street, without giving any hint as to my intentions. One had to he careful all the same.

In the vast number of books written about the secret services of various nations, the job is often made out to consist of highly secret plans and documents being stolen, or more simply photographed by special agents who are able to defy the most complicated systems of protection using science-fiction methods. The results of such exploits, it is given to understand, bring wars to a speedy conclusion in favour of the country with the cleverest spies. In real life these matters, to be frank, are not resolved in such an elementary fashion.

Such confidential plans are available to very few persons and are well guarded. Even plans of general strategy are divided between the heads of various armed forces and the units destined to put them into operation are only instructed at the last moment.

The complete general plan is normally known only to the head of state and two or three high-ranking officers. The usual function of intelligence is to deploy a tight net of observation and close scrutiny of the objectives that have been targeted, to infiltrate all possible channels leading to information on the subject, and to piece together a mosaic so as to form a coherent picture of what is required. Sometimes, by a stroke of luck, an important document may come to hand if it has not been sufficiently protected. It is also possible that military or diplomatic personnel may carelessly blurt out some reserved information carefully recorded by seemingly innocuous hearers. Complete information is seldom available, but a lot of small talk can be pieced together. Patient and careful construction work is always necessary to tie up loose ends.

It was not an easy job to organise the radio listening station in Istanbul, but I had the advantage of being a native and as most of the monitoring staff had to be recruited among the ethnic minorities I was in a favourable position to pick and choose. The listening station was a couple of miles out of town. A powerful motorcar with a driver and bodyguard used to come and fetch me every day, and whenever I walked in town I took care to stay in the middle of the pavement and in full view. It was not safe to walk through solitary, darker and less frequented streets.

In addition to my duties at the listening station I also worked in connection with the United States

Office of War Information and acted as liaison officer between our Intelligence Service and the American set-up. As was to be expected, the Germans had infiltrated our secret service in the same way as we on our part were always informed about everything that was going on at the German Embassy. The subtlest game was to provide the enemy with false information that had all the appearance of credibility.

The Germans employed some Greek typists who professed to be followers of the pro-German party in Greece, but who in reality hated the German invaders of their country. We regularly received their reports. We were not unduly surprised to hear, one day, that secret coded telegrams sent to the American Embassy would appear the next day, duly typed and deciphered, on the desk of one of the secret service agents at the German Embassy. There was undoubtedly a mole at the American Embassy and it was imperative to discover who it was.

Once they had been decoded, reserved messages, with the exception of those marked "Top Secret", were given to a trusted middle-aged secretary who typed them and then distributed them to the four departments concerned. One night soon after, I went to the American Embassy with a lieutenant from the American military intelligence. As we were examining the drawers in the typewriter table used by the secretary, we noticed a stock of freshly used carbon papers. They were new and had only been used to type the day's coded report. Counting the sheets, we noticed five of them had been used, but only four copies were needed.

It did not seem possible that the middle-aged woman was a traitor, as she had been with the embassy for almost twenty years. I started to make very careful enquiries among the secretary's closer friends. She belonged to a good middle-class family of one of the ethnic minorities. It did not take long to hear a tale of woe. The poor woman had a brother in a German concentration camp. She was being blackmailed by the Gestapo and keeping the fact secret from everybody. Every possible care was taken not to alarm the unfortunate secretary who was probably already greatly tormented by her betrayal. We know that she never knew, but that now she is no more, we wish her eternal peace. Thanks to this unexpected good fortune we were able to provide the German secret service with all the "secret information" they thought they were not supposed to know.

The German propaganda machine had organised the war of nerves to a perfect pitch of efficiency. The spreading of false information intended to weaken the morale of the winning enemy troops and the will to resist of the civilian populations was a very powerful weapon of Nazi warfare and had been used to good advantage during and long before the 1935–45 War. The disintegration of the Allied Front which brought about the Dunkerque withdrawal was in a large measure the result of the confusion that was artfully originated by the Germans and their agents, spreading spurious and contradictory information in order to disrupt the Allied resistance opposing their advance.

In England, long before the war, the Nazis had organised a vast network of agents and had used a number of subtle means of propaganda, recruiting to their cause sufficient numbers among the mentally confused pacifists, subversive Irishmen and gullible old women, and feeding them with cleverly distorted information intended to weaken the morale of the British people. The indiscriminate bombing during the first phase of the war against the civilian population, while England was still almost defenceless due to the lack of anti-aircraft armaments, had the effect of counteracting most of this subversive attack on the nation's will to resist. England showed its mettle and the indomitable pride of its people. To counteract the enemy propaganda and this war of nerves we took care not to miss any opportunity to undermine the prestige which the Germans commanded at that time with the non-warring nations as a result of the resounding victories of German troops in the field, which were publicised in every way.

At the beginning of 1944 I heard that a monitor from our Greek section was on very friendly terms with a secretary in the German Embassy. This young man, a pleasant and sociable Viennese, would go often to our monitor's house to talk about the pleasures of life in Vienna, where the old man, our monitor, had spent the best part of his youth. I asked to be invited to have a glass of wine with them, since I, too, remembered happy times in Vienna. Although the secretary knew very well who I was he did not seem to have any ill feelings and talking to each other we discovered some common views about life in general. It did not take long till I finally realised that this Austrian had no love for Nazi Germany and was quite worried to be working with them and exposed to certain danger in the event of a German defeat. As a matter of fact, he had noticed that of late the German armies had lost a large measure of their initial impetus.

I discussed this new connection with the other members of our service at the embassy and we concluded we had to make good of this opportunity by offering to smuggle the young secretary, out of the blue, across the frontier into Egypt where he would be out of the war and safe against any reprisals which might be taken against him as a Nazi, after we had won the war. The young man agreed and disappeared from the German Embassy one fine morning. It could be thought that his desertion might have provided us with information that was not already known to us, but our purpose was quite different. Making use of subtle systems of divulgation, the Turkish papers came to know of this fact and there was a lot of noise made about it, since thanks to the vivid imagination of newspapermen, the rumour was spread that the embassy secretary had run away to our side taking with him a large sum in gold bullion which was kept at the German

Embassy to pay their secret agents. Since mice are the first to leave a sinking ship, the event was taken to indicate that Germany's chances of victory were failing and German prestige in Turkey took a hard blow.

Some time after I had been posted to Istanbul our agents informed us across the border, in the Balkan countries, that the Germans were concentrating hundreds of gliders on Bulgarian airfields. It was not difficult to conclude that the enemy was planning to attack our armies in the Near East, using Turkish territory as a jumping board. I did not suppose it would be a walkover for them altogether to convince the Turks. Therefore, some days after the information had somehow reached public knowledge, and to show Turkey's resolution not to be involved, there was an important demonstration of military strength. Large numbers of troops were transported across the water from the Asiatic side to the European part of Istanbul, where the most important airfield was situated. What finally put a stop to the Germans' plans was the dropping, at Varna, of a thousand Russian paratroops who held the port for several days. Bulgarian resistance fighters were considerably bolstered by this action and they started to burn gliders on the airfields. I think it was as a sequel to these events that lukewarm Bulgaria finally decided to get out of the Axis and abandon the war. We heard the news late one night at our listening station, which was manned at all hours. We transmitted the information immediately to the War Office in London, hot as it had come.

I remained for a few months more at Istanbul and then went back to Cairo, to join my comrades at the section. It was September 1945. The war in Europe had ended and we expected to be demobilised very soon and sent back home. I was very anxious to take a trip to Milan in order to find out about the state of my business, which I had left in the care of my partner on leaving Italy. Soon, I thought, I would go back to civilian life with all of its everyday problems.

I went to see the officer in charge of air transport at General Headquarters in Cairo. He was a very nice person and explained to me that transport by air, from one military zone to another, was only possible if there were particular orders for posting. Exceptions were made, of course, for General Staff officers, with red tabs, who did not need any justification to obtain an air passage. I explained to him that I had no such orders. Then, as he was very willing to talk, he asked me why I was so anxious to fly to Milan. I told him that my profession concerned Oriental antiques and I wanted to find out whether my prized possessions still existed. At the word Oriental antiques, a wide smile spread over his rotund face.

"I am a lecturer in Oriental archaeology, myself," he said and we immediately lapsed in a conversation about the things we both loved. It seemed to me as if we were both out of uniform, he lecturing on his platform and I in my gallery, pouring out knowledge and wisdom to our respective audiences. As I was going away he said to me, "Don't worry, old boy. If any of the big brass decides to change his plans about his passage, I'll let you know."

Two days went by and my friend called me over the phone. "Be at the airport tomorrow at seven o'clock."

I had no problem in leaving the section for a few days. We were all one big family. The plane was an old Dakota and the pilot was South African. It was the first time I had ever flown. One did not travel very much by air before the war. There were six passengers, sitting on hard benches leaning against the sides of the aircraft. A New Zealand air force lieutenant who had been transferred to Milan sat next to me. There was a jeep waiting for him when we arrived at the airport and he gave me a lift into town. It was a fortunate opportunity, as I do not know how I would have reached the city otherwise. There was no transport available for me.

As we arrived in Piazza San Babila I looked in vain for the entrance to Via Montenapoleone where I wanted to be dropped. I had told the young lieutenant that Milan was my home and I felt very embarrassed not to be able to direct the driver of the jeep properly. I had to ask a passer-by. During my years of absence the part of Via Montenapoleone that was at right angles to Corso Vittorio Emanuele had been cut away. The intersection was now a large square. I got down from the jeep in front of my shop. My partner was at the back and had no view on the street. When he caught sight of me all of a sudden he almost gasped with emotion. He was a very good person, much older than I. We had been in partnership for a long time and remained together later, for over twenty years.

One of my wife's sisters lived in Milan, with her husband, son and daughter. They, too, were amazed to hear my voice on the phone, all so unexpectedly. They had returned to Italy a short while before, after having taken refuge in Switzerland, escaping from Nazi persecution, through the barbed wire of the mountain frontier. My nephew came to fetch me with his big bicycle. We loaded my suitcase onto his bike and went home on foot. There were no taxis.

Milan was a sad sight in September 1945. Gutted buildings stood half-destroyed all over the city and the circular road, which had been built over the Naviglio Grande, was lined on both sides with ruined buildings and tall mounds of rubble. The pale faces of the people, the almost total absence of road traffic, the stumps of the beautiful trees that had lined the alleys, all told a long story of deprivation.

I went the rounds of my friends: the hairdresser, the tailor, and the owner of the stationery shop next door to mine. I felt at home and all of a sudden, the military period of my life, into which I had fitted to the extent of forgetting that I had lived differently before, began to seem like an episode that had already ended. The people I knew and met in the street welcomed me with joy. My uniform did not seem to disturb them. The war was over and everybody wanted to forget about it.

I was waiting for one of the rare tramways one morning in Via Manzoni when I noticed a wizened old man of poor appearance who was muttering to himself not far from where I stood. He was looking at me askance. I thought he was puzzled by my uniform, but I finally realised that I was the object of his scorn. A few minutes went by and he moved from where he was and trudged slowly in front of me.

"Go home, you devil, go home," I heard him mumble in Milanese dialect as he passed by, looking down at his feet.

I hardly suppressed my laughter and answered him loudly and cheerily in the same idiom: "Wish I could, old man. I'm browned off, as it is." My tram had finally arrived and I had to look sharp. I wish I could have seen the old man's face as I was pushed into the throng.

My ten days' leave had gone by like lightning. I had to get back to Cairo but I had some trouble getting an air passage from Milan. All I could do was to get to Bari with a group of officers on transfer. I was not on official business. My visit to Milan appeared to be purely accidental. The major in charge of air transport at Bari was a hard nut to crack. He was haughty and unpleasant. He wanted to send me back to Egypt on a cargo ship, which was leaving for Alexandria three days later. I did not like that at all. I had not spent five years in the army without learning a thing or two.

As he repeated his refusal to grant me a passage by air, I said to him very coldly: "All right, Sir, if it is all the same to you and you wish to assume responsibility and answer to my unit for keeping me here for so many days. I suppose you are aware that an Intelligence officer does not travel without a purpose."

I did not risk much with this piece of cheek. Had he sent a message to General Headquarters in Cairo, the head of our section would have put things right. We were the spoilt children of the Political Intelligence Centre and enjoyed great privilege. I had my passage the same day and my comrades and I had a good laugh about my performance in Bari. We were at the end of 1945. We felt now that military life was definitely over. We were going back to our civilian occupations, back to the world we had abandoned five years before when we had put aside everything which bound us with our past existence. Now, slowly, day by day, the memory of the home I had left was growing more distinct and forceful. I was now allowing the image of my wife, which I had willingly blurred in my mind, to become vivid again. At last, late in November, we received orders to embark for England. We crossed the Mediterranean in a large troopship. There were still floating mines about and I remember thinking it would be such a pity to die now that it was all over and I was going home.

We disembarked in Toulon. The port was a cemetery for the French warships that had been scuttled by their crews. We were held up for three days in a transit camp by unceasing rain. The people in the town did not hide their ill feelings against their British ally.

We finally left this unfriendly place, travelling by train across France, crowded to the utmost in third-class carriages in a long, slow convoy. As we reached the coast on the Channel all discomfort was forgotten. We were really going home. On the ferry everyone was on the decks trying to be the first to make out, through the mist, the familiar outline of the country we had left for so many difficult years, and when the cliffs of Dover finally appeared in sight, many an eye was moist with a suppressed tear.

We handed back our weapons and kit at the demobilisation centre near Dover and were issued with a suitcase containing a set of civilian clothes. I confess I was sad to think I would have to abandon my uniform. I had worn it with pride, very conscious of its meaning to me. It represented the fulfilment of my bounden duty to the nation of which I considered myself part.

I took a train to Manchester. My wife had come back to live there with our good friends who had given her a home all through the war. The house they lived in was in a quiet neighbourhood, in a short street lined with villas and well-kept gardens. I rang at the door. It was getting dark and the light under the porch was rather dim. There she was on the threshold. We looked at each other in silence. It all seemed to be happening in a dream. We fell into each other's arms. So much time had gone by and I had done my best to keep my wife's physical presence constrained in the back of my memory in order to lessen the ache I felt of not being with her. Now, as I looked again at her face, listened to her voice and felt her body, the love and affection, which I had kept dormant, surged back again in renewed happiness.

As the war ended my wife and I decided we would go back to Italy. Seven years had elapsed since we had left the country. Seven hard years that had disrupted the course of our life and changed our way of thinking. I was now brought face to face again with the problems of daily life from which I had been distanced, like so many others under the same circumstances who had to abandon themselves entirely to providence, as they went into service for their warring nations. The war period, the severance from problems of work had, in many instances, brought a new insight into one's conscience, an awareness of the servitude that bound one to a job or profession, imposed by the necessity of earning a living. Many often asked themselves, at this stage, why follow a way that had been decided upon, more by circumstances than by one's own choice.

The interest I had always had in my profession did not place me in any such quandary and I resumed my former activity with renewed energy, trying to bring to it more knowledge, and aiming for higher standards of art. My continuous peregrinations from one school to another during my formative years, and the different languages and teaching methods had considerably enriched and widened my knowledge of general world history. At a time when comparative history had not yet been included in the school curriculum, my lessons at these different schools had helped to form a coherent picture of historical events in relation to the various European countries involved in my studies.

As far as I remember, I had always nurtured, even in my early youth, a keen interest for antiques and *objets d'art*, coupled with a never-ending curiosity about their origins and history. Our home was full of interesting objects and beautiful carpets, which had been inherited by my guardian from his grandfather or which he had collected himself with great zest. In doing so, he had acted like so many physicians who see this pastime as way of escaping, for a while, from the dire reality of their profession, which puts them in daily contact with the saddest and most pitiless sides of life.

We had beautiful blue and white Chinese porcelain, antique Oriental silver objects, artistically embossed and nielloed, damascene swords with gold or silver sheaths covered with precious and semi-precious stones. We also had seventeenth- and eighteenth-century English furniture, which were part of the large consignments of such articles that my great-grandfather imported for the Sultan's palaces, for which he was an authorised purveyor.

In addition to all this, our home was covered with rare carpets on the floors and often on the walls, for choice pieces. I somehow felt very attracted by carpets. I suppose I was sensitive to their beautiful colours.

At the English High School for Boys where I was finishing my studies, a singular circumstance seemed to have given me an indication as to the profession I would enter finally as a result of the unforeseen developments of my life. A prize competition for an essay on the British Empire was sponsored by the chairman of an English bank in the city. The prize money was ten pounds sterling, which was a lot in those days. I was by far the youngest competitor and when it was decreed I had written the best essay, the headmaster had qualms about putting so much money into the hands of a sixteen-year-old youngster. As a logical alternative, the decision was taken to buy three expensive books to be distributed to the second and third candidates as well. The three titles were: an anthology of English Literature, an illustrated history of Byzantium and the *Practical Handbook of Oriental Carpets* by G. Friffin Lewis, which had recently been published in 1921. I had first choice and I took the book on carpets. I still treasure it with its dedication from the headmaster, dated 1922.

There were quite a good number of well-stocked antique shops around our home. The most important luxury hotel, called the Pera Palace, stood in all its majesty, right opposite our building. The antique dealers had chosen this location in the hope of luring into their shops some of the wealthy foreigners who patronised the hotel. Most of these shopkeepers knew my uncle who was their good customer and when I started to wander into their premises with my prize-book under my arm, they had an indulgent smile for me and were always ready to give me some explanations.

At that time not much was known about the history of carpets. Antique dealers in Constantinople in those days had only a practical and instinctive knowledge of the goods they dealt in, but this fact did not in the least make them unable to judge, at first glance, the importance of the treasures which were often offered to them for sale. These antique shops were an enchanted world for me and I often ask myself now why I was so attracted to these things at an age when a growing youngster ought to dream about so many other pastimes. When, in later life, the course of events brought me into contact with the commercial side of Oriental carpets, I had a fair knowledge of the matter, but I was always more attracted by the older pieces that sometimes came our way. I tried as much as possible to discover more about the origin and the period of these antique carpets at a time when little literature was available on this subject. Carpet weaving is now an area of such meticulous and scientific research that it risks losing much of its mystery.

Studying antique carpets brought me gradually to form an interest in other aspects of Oriental art.

I think this happened mainly because my memory was crowded with the beautiful Oriental antiques that surrounded my early youth, in our home in Turkey. The thirst for knowledge never abates. Being in contact with beautiful artefacts, which one can examine at will and touch with sensitive hands, brings to life more vividly their history than reading about them in art books.

I have always been a diligent visitor of museums during my travels and I was particularly interested in antique carpet collections in these museums. I had to look and try to understand since there was little to be learned from books written on carpets at the time. Proffered notions were rather vague and inconsistent. In order to form an opinion one had to rely on experience, instinct and sensitivity, on shades of colour and above all visual memory. The notions one acquired on the history of those Oriental countries where carpets had been woven over the centuries were also very useful, when encountered.

I still remember with unabated gratification, an episode that took place in Istanbul, a couple of years before the war when I was on a visit to my in-laws who lived there. It was in 1937, a few months after I was married. I was visiting the Evkaf Oriental Carpet Museum,[13] which was situated in those days in the vicinity of the Grand Bazaar, and was going

---

[13] This is now known as the Türk ve İslam Eserleri Museum, or Museum of Turkish and Islamic Art.

through the rooms when I met a middle-aged gentleman, an acquaintance of mine, who was one of the managers of an important Oriental carpet firm in London. We were looking at the displayed carpets together and I, who even at that time professed to be an expert on antique carpets, was holding forth on a group of sixteenth-century Ushak carpets, when I suddenly noticed among the pieces close to each other on the wall, an Ushak carpet which I reckoned was at least a century older than the other pieces owing to its particular shades of colour and varied pattern.

My friend, very conscious of his exalted position and wide experience, would not share my judgement and we were discussing the matter rather loudly, when I felt a light hand on my shoulder. I turned around and found myself face to face with a distinguished old gentleman with a white beard.

"I am the curator of this museum," he said, "and I wish to congratulate you, my young friend, for your sensitive knowledge of Oriental carpets. I would like to put an offer to you if I may. There are eight hundred antique carpets in our basement, which still have to be classified. It is a long and tiresome task; I am old and I cannot think of completing it without aid. Would you be prepared to help me?"

Although this unexpected and flattering offer sent thrills of pride down my spine, I told the old gentleman that although I would willingly do it, I had to return to Italy to attend to my business.

As we proceeded through the various halls, I noticed a series of seventeenth-century so-called Isfahan carpets, which in some instances revealed a marked Caucasian influence in their patterns. I inferred, as seemed very plausible, that there must have been an influx, at that period, of Armenian people in the Isfahan region. I told my friend about it but he was already sick and tired of my pretentiousness and replied that I was nurturing fanciful dreams. I was a greenhorn compared to him, in age and experience.

Some years later, I came across a pamphlet published in Austria that dealt with the influence of the Armenians on the patterns of seventeenth-century Isfahan carpets. When the Christian Armenians fled from their native country, hard pressed by the Turkish invaders, a considerable number of them had established themselves near Isfahan, across the river Arax, in a township they had called New Djulfa. Peoples' histories are often more clearly written in their artefacts than they are in historians' chronicles.

One of the more satisfying prerogatives of an antiquarian is to be able to identify, by instinct and observation, an object he does not know and that he has never seen before. For him it is the crowning of his knowledge, the result of his experience, the reward of his studies. It gives him the gratification of having resolved a difficult problem. To his visual awareness he soon adds a tactile sensitivity.

It is hardly possible to establish familiarity without understanding an object's smoothness, its patina or the velvety finish of its texture. Fingers serve as a corollary to the eye and awaken in the mind an echo of cognizance. With time one may sometimes also develop an aptitude to sense the message which is hidden in those few inspiring works of art, which are the figment of an artist's creative power at the moment when he is possessed by an overpowering stimulus, one that he is unable to define, but which carries him over and above human endeavour.

Those who are not sensitive enough to recognise such creative wonders have surely missed intense moments of joy. He who does not feel a thrill of rare pleasure at the sight of an exceptional work of art, who is not moved to tears when he feels on his skin the creative breath of the artist, and the divine inspiration which underlies the immortal work of art, does not enjoy to the full the gift with which he may have been endowed by Nature, although the latter does not always act as a foster-mother to all humans. On a trip to India some years ago, while I was visiting the exceptional museum in Sarnath, I found myself looking intently at a wonderful sculpture, a Buddha of the Gupta period, sitting in meditation. Suddenly a lump came into my throat and tears welled into my eyes. I could not restrain myself and was ashamed, for people were looking at me with curiosity. It does not often happen that one falls prey to such intense and overpowering feelings, but there are certain works of art that affect sensitive people very deeply.

Years ago, we had in our gallery a figure of Buddha, a Japanese wooden sculpture of the sixteenth century, which seemed to come forward towards its onlookers. This statue gave out such tremendous power that it was not possible to look at it for long without being forcefully affected by its hypnotic compulsion. We had to keep it in a closed niche. One day a Japanese psychologist, a very cultured person and a selective collector, came to visit our gallery. I took him to see the Buddha. As I opened the closet where the statue was hidden, I saw this gentleman stiffen in an attitude of devotion and stand for a couple of minutes in meditation. As he resumed his normal attitude, he bowed three times in reverence and walking backwards asked me to please shut the door of the niche again. I was deeply impressed and though brought up by my creed not to venerate man-made images, I could understand the mystic power that was given out by this wonderful sculpture, which was undoubtedly created by its artist in a moment of divine communion.

An antiquarian must travel and know the world. He must look at what surrounds him and he is perhaps more receptive to outside influence because of his experience and the training he has acquired in his profession. He comes back from his wanderings with a wealth of lasting images, enriched with new knowledge and with the advantage of having known and established human contact with people who live and think in a different way. His travels are like an open vista on the outside world, but his natural habitat is within his place of work. He lives in it as in a shell, immersed in the past. His very nature resents the influx of the surrounding atmosphere. He is not easily involved in the present. People who come to see him are influenced by the same serenity that pervades the atmosphere and are often prepared to engage in an unconstrained dialogue.

During the fifty years or more that I have exercised my profession I have known many people. Passers-by who happened to walk in one day have become lifelong friends with whom I have shared what I knew and above all the philosophy of life I have gathered over these many years. I have often divided with them the exalting feeling one experiences at the sight of human achievement when it soars above individual possibilities and touches the fibres of the soul. I have also learned much from those who came.

And now the days have gone with the passing years and I give thanks for the gift of life, for the joys of the family, for the ancestral tradition which has taught me to do right and to help my neighbour, for the clear sky and the sun's splendour, for the green meadows and the dark woods, for the little birds that sing in the trees at dawn, for the water that gushes so fresh from the fountain in the summer's heat, and for all the wonders of Creation which kindle in our hearts the belief in God.

> *Time has passed, but I have no regrets for what I have not done or will no longer do. When life comes towards the end, one stops looking ahead because the road has already been eventful. Old wounds cease to hurt and memories soften and lighten the spirit.*